SCENES OF
EARLIER DAYS

In Crossing the Plains to Oregon, and Experiences of Western Life

by
CHARLES HOWARD CRAWFORD

AMERICANA CLASSICS
QUADRANGLE BOOKS, INC.
Chicago
584172

First edition published 1898, Petaluma, California
This edition published 1962 by
Quadrangle Books, Inc. / Chicago

———————

Library of Congress Catalog Card Number: 62-12188

MANUFACTURED IN THE UNITED STATES OF AMERICA
BY BOOK CRAFTSMEN ASSOCIATES, INC., NEW YORK

PREFACE.

@HOSE who did not cross the plains, either to Oregon or California, in an early day have but little knowledge of the hardships endured by the way, or after their arrival at their future homes. I have frequently conversed with those who went to Oregon from 1843 to 1845 and '46 and after their arrival had to live on acorns for six weeks without meat. There were no cattle at the time in the country fit for beef, and game was very scarce, and even if it had been plenty hunting it on an acorn breakfast would have been very hard work

Even after our arrival in Oregon at a later date, 1851, provisions were very scarce. The winter of 1852-53 for more than a month there was no flour to be had and no meat and we paid $8.50 for fifty pounds of very poor shorts and glad to get it at that price. In the spring a cargo of Chile flour came in and when we bought it we had to sieve out the long woolly worms and eat it or starve. In talking with friends about the scenes of earlier days and experiences of western life I have been frequently asked why do you not write them out and have them published in book form. My reply has been it always looked egotistical for a man to publish his own autobiography The reply was this is not your autobiography, but actual history that helps to tell about the settlement of the great west, a subject in which old and young are, or should be, deeply interested. Setting all objections aside I submit in the following pages an account of our trip across the plains together with a few

of our varied experiences of western life in the hope
that it will do at least a small amount of good in bettering the great state in which we live.

The scenes related in this book are true for I was an
eye witness to most of them. Many of them were of a
nature to stir up the soul with intense excitement.
I shall be glad to know that the young people who read
these truthful narratives have been benefitted by them.
Those who love truth more than fiction will not object
to these sketches.

C. H. CRAWFORD,

PETALUMA, Cal., 1898.

CONTENTS.

Scenes of Early Days.

THE START MADE.

CHAPTER I.

Our minds are so formed that we love to linger around the scenes of the past and think of what transpired in years gone by. How often have we been charmed with the company of the aged ones as they related to us the things that transpired when they were young. The struggle they had, the difficulties they overcame and their final triumph at the last when they proved conquerors. Many a youth in our land has felt a noble thrill in his soul when grandma or grandpa has talked about frontier life in the wilderness, and told their experiences with bears, wolves and wild Indians. Not only do old people have their attractions, but also old buildings, that have long been erected and have stood the storms of many years.

I have visited Fort Ross in the western portion of Sonoma county, California, and on the border of the Pacific ocean, and looked with deep interest on the walls now tumbling into ruins and thought of the struggles through which the Russians must have passed when they were built, surrounded as they were with wild beasts and wilder savages. Their struggles were but little if any greater than those who settled our western frontier, going forth with their loaded muskets in one hand and the torch of liberty in the other. Those who are now being whirled across the continent with the onward rush of the railroad coach. often wonder how the emigrants of earlier days ever made their way to the Pacific coast, in the midst of savages, mosquitoes, black gnats and alkali dust. I never felt any alarm about our western travel until I made the trip some years after the railroad was completed, and saw the old emigrant road as it came in sight occasionally. Then it was the past loomed up and I thought it was a very risky business to take a family (for their were four of us) and start out on a western trip of more than two thousand miles, and depend on four horses and a wagon to bring us to our "desired heaven," with nothing for feed for our animals save the grass we migt find by the way. Then add to this that we had to travel outside of civilization on a road not improved, and cross swollen streams as best we could, and not see a house from the Missouri river to Oregon, save at the forts, and you will not wonder that it made me almost shudder as my thoughts surveyed the past.

It was April 10, 1851, when a small company left the western portion of Illinois, to make the trip across the western wilds to Oregon. As the company formed and moved away from their old homes, an old gentleman who was traveling with us remarked: "Westward the star of empire wends its way." We crossed the Mississippi at the town (now the city of Burlington) and made our way across Iowa, the western portion then being very thinly settled. We halted for several days at a place now known as Council Bluffs, then Council Bluffs was two or three miles farther up the Missouri river. The reason we tarried here was to let the grass grow, so that it would have more strength for our horses. The emigrants kept on coming until thousands were encamped on the borders of the river. As we were traveling with horses, without any cattle, we were desirous of forming a good company in numbers so as to pass in safety through the Pawnee country, as they were said to be somewhat troublesome. By hunting among the various camps of emigrants we soon found enough with horses to make a company of one hundred and twenty men, well armed, besides women and children. A day was set when we were to meet and organize and determine when we were to cross the muddy Missouri. The day arrived, and an organization was affected by the election of a Mr. Hadley as our captain, as he had crossed the plains in 1849 in search of California gold.

CHAPTER II.

The day selected for the forward journey was a delightful one and the 6th day of May found us, without a single accident, on the west side of the great river where the beautiful city of Omaha now stands. Then there were no signs of civilization not even a log cabin had been reared. Out west of this a few miles there were the remnants of a few cabins to be seen, where some Mormons on their way to Salt Lake had wintered a few years before. We found our first camping place on the Elk Horn and after we had found our camp a few Indians came to us. They were hard-featured human beings and looked wicked enough for any mischief. They were clad in buffalo robes and by moving them up and down they made a horrid rattling noise, which greatly frightened our teams and they started to run, for prior to this they had been unhitched and were eating grass. Those who saw this movement on the part of the Indians and the stampede of the horses, succeeded in turning all back except three of mine and they ran at full speed out on to the plains. Some of those who were fortunate enough to keep their horses from running, mounted them and after a chase of several miles all were brought back safely. The Indians were notified that if they scared the horses again they would be punished severely for it. They remained very quiet during the night, camping not far from us

The next morning we journeyed on until we found a stream called Loup Fork which was so greatly swollen that the ferryman told us we would have to wait several days before crossing. We paid him $5 so as to secure our regular time of crossing. We moved up the river where there was better grass, and the ferryman promised he would let us know when it was safe to cross. One day while waiting for the waters to fall we saw another train drive up and commence crossing. We harnessed our teams as quickly as possible, and moved down to the ferry and demanded our time as promised. The ferryman said, "gentlemen, you must settle your own troubles, as the last train to arrive has paid me ten dollars to cross it first." A man at least six feet tall stepped forth from the last train and said "he would fight any man in our train, and let that decide the matter." An Englishman in our company of small statue, but who proved to be a scientific boxer, said "sir, I am your man." The captain said, "form a ring, gentlemen and let them fight." The ring was soon formed, while the women and children remained in the wagons as witnesses of the scene, but by no means as disinterested spectators, for all were anxious to push foward as soon as possible.

CHAPTER III.

The two combatants having placed themselves in the proper position, the captain of each company called to his man "are you ready?" They both declared they were, the word was given and the tall man made for the Englishman, swinging both of his arms wildly in the air. In the meantime the Englishman scarcely moved from his position, but as his man came up he watched his opportunity and placed a blow on his chest which knocked him down, without himself receiving a scratch. The Englishman stood back and waited for his man to get up. After awhile he rolled his eyes up as if pleading for help, at the same time saying he was not whipped yet. "Get up then," said the Englishman, "I will give you all you want." With the assistance of some of his comrades he got up and steadied himself for a short time, and then declared he could and would whip his antagonist. He made at him as before, swinging his arms in all directions. The Englishman stood still in order to receive his blows, and when he came near enough he landed a left-hand blow just below the ear, and he fell as suddenly as if stabbed to the heart. He never struck the Englishman a single lick, and he was struck only twice, but they were blows that counted. When he fell the second time quite a number thought he was killed, but after awhile he showed some signs of life, and his comrades helped him up and carried him to his wagon. We learned afterward that he kept his bed for three weeks before he was able to move about at his own will. The only injury the Englishman sustained was a badly sprained thumb on the left hand, caused by the last blow he struck.

After the fight was over, the tall man's captain said: "Gentlemen you have won it fairly, it is your right to cross the Loup Fork first." We soon shoved a wagon on the boat, and after a few hours we all landed safely on the west side. I suppose this fight was on the same principle, only in a small degree, that causes nations to go to war with each other. Trouble arises and one is

offended and seeks revenge. The spirit of retaliation
is very strongly marked in some individuals as well as
in some nations. All hands, men, women and children
were very much interested in this fight, for all were
anxious to be moving westward. This was a war
on a small scale, while it lasted. It was a very
decisive battle, and one that accomplished its work and
left the ferry free to us. Such scenes these days I think
are frowned on by the better class of society, but then
it was thought to be about right, as church members,
class leaders and a parson helped to form the ring, and
as good as said: "Go in boys and do your best, to the
victor belongs the spoils."

Opinions on many subjects are undergoing as great
changes these days, as the country has through which
we were then passing. Now fine cities, towns and
farms dot the road we were then traveling, and the fiery
steed goes puffing along his iron track, and the people
are rejoicing in plenty, with no fear of being molested
by the Indian tribes who once inhabited it, and roamed
over its hills and valleys, at their own will and pleasure.
I am glad that the great principles of peace are taking a
firmer hold on the human heart as well as on nations
who before have been blood thirsty. When Nellie Bly
was in Mexico, a Spanish gentleman said to her: "Your
humane societies would prevent bull fights in the
States. Your people would cry out against them. Yet
they have strong men trying to pound one another
to death, and the people clamor for admission to see the
law kill men and women, while in health and in youth,
because of some deed done in the flesh. Yes, they wit-

ness and allow such inhuman treatment to a fellow mortal, and turn around and affect holy horror at us for taking out of the world a few old horses and furnishing beef to the poor " A point, I think, very well taken by the Spanish gentleman.

Forty-seven years ago and railroads were not very plentiful, much less one to traverse the western wilds, and cross hills and tall ranges of mountains, and find its way puffing and snorting to the great Pacific. I remember very well when plows had wooden mold boards, and harvesting was done with reap hooks, and then with cradles. With the vast and far reaching improvements now in use, we must naturally expect ideas to change, and men become more manly by leaving off their childish notions. But I am wandering from my theme and must return.

We traveled up the north side of Platt river, and for quite a distance our route seemed quite level. There was a new difficulty which was soon encountered by us, for we now had a stretch of three hundred miles without and wood with which to make fires and do our cooking.

CHAPTER IV.

The question of how the cooking was to be done was to all of us a very important one, but it was very soon settled by our captain telling us that we had to use buffalo chips, and that we must camp where they were the most plentiful. It was amusing to see the different expressions of countenance when this announcement was made. Ladies who had been reared in luxury and were generally noted for their good nature and mild manners, fairly stamped the earth and almost gritted their teeth together, declaring they never could and never would cook with it, that they would rather retrace their steps and live on the east side of the Missouri river, or then eat their vituals raw and use cold water for coffee. But traveling soon produces strong appetites, and hunger with its gnawings is not easily satisfied with raw food, and it was only a short time until, when the train halted for either noon or night, men, women and children made haste to the field of chips and gathered them for fuel, and even the ladies who had said so much, were as eager to procure the driest as any of the rest. The women soon learned to cook with them, and all hands became used to such fuel; really the vituals seemed to taste just as good as if cooked with wood. It is an excellent thing we are so formed that we can adapt ourselves to the surrounding circumstances. If this was not true there would be but few who would ever see the western wilds, or the immense west as we used to call it. From start to finish, western travel a half century ago was a kind of rough and tumble life, with difficulties in abundance, but we soon learned to sleep in tents, wagons or on the ground, and to eat our gruel cooked with buffalo manure. And here I will say lest I forget it further on, that ladies, and even those who never knew what hardships were at home, can endure more of them in proportion to their strength than men. When men become discouraged and are ready to faint by the way, their courage comes to the rescue and urges the men forward.

There is some very beautiful country bordering on the Platte river, with a large extent of good level land, and as we traveled up this beautiful valley, in the distance we could see vast herds of buffalo feeding, which at times would become alarmed at our covered wagons and scamper off out of our sight to the rolling hills. There are some countries beautiful to look upon when the sun shines brightly, and no angry clouds are to be seen. So it proved with the Platte. for I remember one day, the forenoon had been all that heart could wish, when suddenly a cloud angry in its contour came up and the hail commenced to fall. I had to get out of the wagon with its covered shelter and hold my leaders by the bits to keep them from running away. Hail stones fell larger than quails eggs, by the thousand and pelted my hands, until black and blue for days. How that portion of our country now is, since it has been crossed and recrossed with railroads and towns and cities have been built, I do not know; but then it was by far the worst country I ever have been in for storms. I have passed through some very hard storms in Illinois, but none that would do to compare with those along the Platte.

One I remember very vividly. The day had been very warm and at times quite sultry. We camped for the night on a small stream running into the main river, and after our suppers were ate and the guards placed on duty for the night, the distant thunders began with their rumbling noise, when nearer they came with their forked lightnings playing hither and thither, until at last a mighty crash broke loose that seemed to shake the very earth and arose the entire camp. Although no moon shone, yet such was the power of the electric current that human faces could be seen in plain outline, and at times a pin might have been seen on the ground. I suppose one reason it seemed so bad to us was that we were in a dreary wilderness surrounded by savages, with no opportunity to secure help even if we wanted it very badly. Then add to this, the fact that we had to picket all our horses and stake all our wagons with ropes, so as to keep them from being blown away, and our horses from running before the storm. Such were the wild scenes of that night that the entire company was filled with solemn awe and made to wonder whether we were to encounter many scenes like this on our westward journey. Our captain to encourage us said he never had encountered such a night as this in all his travels.

The next day after this storm was the sabbath, and as we journeyed on I saw a man some distance from the road sitting in the door of his tent who looked quite familiar. This man was also a parson, crossing with an ox train. Before leaving his eastern home he had urged this trip, saying that he thought it would add at least fifteen years to a man's life to cross the plains to Oregon. As soon as I recognized him fully I called out to him: "Uncle Neil Johnson is not this a rather hard way to add fifteen years to a man's life." His long sad Sunday face instantly relaxed into smiles as he saw who I was, and came forward with extended hand and as I

I saw a man some distance from the road sitting in the door of his tent.—page 11

grasped it he said: "I rather think it is for I never bargained for so much." When I came to talk with him I found that during the wild night of which I have spoken, his cattle stampeded and he was left with only one yoke of cattle to pull his three wagons and family to Oregon. I learned afterwards that his sons, who were out searching for the cattle when I was at his tent, found them all, and from that on he was as fortunate as most of the emigrants. Afer we all arrived safely in Oregon, he used to tell of our meeting that day on the Platte, and how I made sport about adding fifteen years to a man's life not knowing at the time he had lost his cattle in the storm.

One day, as we were traveling leisurely along, all at once several hundred Pawnee Indians came dashing up to our train on their bobtail ponies with their faces all painted in war style.

CHAPTER V.

They came with a war whoop. no doubt with the hopes of frightening us. But as we numbered one hundred and twenty men and showed them our military arms they said they only wanted pay for passing through their country. We even refused this for our captain had told us not to pay them anything, nor give them anything to eat. When they saw they could gain nothing from us they left peaceably and went after some ox trains, where they were more successful in their efforts as they obtained a three year old heifer from one company.

It was while traveling in the Platte country that I saw
my first hare, or what we as Californians now call "jack
rabbits." In company with a friend who was known as
Joe Lucas in our train, I went out one day some distance
from the road to hunt for game. Just as we began to
enter the foot hills up jumped an animal with very long
ears for its height or the length of its body, as it started
from us it seemed to be lame. After a few jumps it
stood on its hind legs and looked at us as much as to
say, "I dare you to fire a shot at me." I raised my gun
to fire, but, as hunters say, it snapped, for by some
means the powder was damp. When I found my gun
was a failure I called out, "Joe, shoot it, or it will get
away from us yet." "No," said he, "I will catch it
for it is very lame and cannot run far." He seated himself, pulled off his boots and socks and away he went
on the chase. The animal made a few leaps and was
out of sight, lame as he seemed to be.

It would be hard to picture a more forlorn looking
man than Joe was when he seated himself to pull the
stickers out of his feet and put on his boots. Said he
"I never was so deceived in an animal in all my life."
What can it be, anyway.

He was as much disappointed as the Irishman who
came to America and had never seen much of the world.
I do not vouch for the truthfulness of this story, but
give it to you just as I heard it.

As I said the Irishman came to America and landed
in San Francisco but as he was raised on a farm he made
his way into the country to look for work. One day he
met a man driving a pair of mules and his wagon was

loaded with large squashes.   He ventured up to the
driver and said (putting his hand on the squashes)
"What are these things?"   "These," said the driver,
are mule eggs and if you want to raise an animal like
these I am driving all you have to do is to take one of
these eggs and set on it for three weeks and it will
hatch out a mule.

Pat took one and sat on it until he became tired and
then went away for a rest. While he was gone a jack
rabbitt hid himself behind it and when Pat returned the
animal jumped up and ran off.   Gazing after it and
seeing its long ears he instantly called out, "Hey, you
baste, come back here. I am your father."

We were not quite as green as Pat, but one thing
sure we did not know the name of the animal, and the
fact was it looked like a mule with its long ears.

The first buffalo we saw on our travels was on the
Platte, and a number of our men concluded one day, as
a beautiful herd came in sight, that they would give
chase and secure some fresh meat if possible.   Some
went with horses and some on foot. They wandered so
far from the train that day that only those on horses
could return.   The footmen remained out without food
or blankets.   Neither were successful in their hunt and
we had to abide our time for fresh meat.

The second day in the afternoon the footmen caught
up with us, tired and foot sore.   One of the footmen
whose name was Bill Havens, at least called such among
the boys, had a most marvelous tale to relate of his ad-
ventures and narrow escapes. He said, "I got near
enough to shoot a buffalo and it made him mad and he

took after me. When the others saw him running they ran too and I was chased by a large herd. They were all throwing their tails 'wiggletree, waggletree, wiggletree, waggletree.' "

It seemed so unreasonable that one could see the tails of an entire herd of buffalo when he was running for dear life with all his speed from them, that all who heard him laughed heartily. An old gentleman in the train, who had been a member of the Illinois legislature for eight terms in succession, called out "attention, men, this man's name shall be Buffalo Bill from this on, for he is the only man living that could run from a herd of buffalo and at the same time see their tails going wiggletree, waggletree."

He carried that name into Oregon and I heard of him afterward in California and he still kept the name. It was said that he carried the name back to Michigan, the state from whence he came, but whether he did or not he was a useful man in the company and ever ready to lend a helping hand. He was not the Buffalo Bill of the Wild West shows.

In our journeying one day we saw a very tall object rearing its head above valleys and hills and we knew from what we had read and what our captain told us that it must be Chimney rock. We found when we attempted to measure distances in that country with the eye we were very liable to be greatly deceived. Some thought it might be ten miles distant, some fifteen, while a few others said it might be twenty. Some of our party resolved to see it and they started very early in the morning traveling all day and camping out.

CHAPTER VI.

It was not until the second day that they reached it, and to their surprise and chagrin found that it had been a very large rock and that the teeth of time had been gnawing on it until in the distance it looked like a chimney There was an immense pile of rock at the foot that had been broken off and fallen down, while a mere stem was left standing.

The men were out three days and two nights to see a huge mass of stone, and to travel what some thought was ten, fifteen or twenty miles. This cured them of going off great distances in order to see the curiosities by the way.

Traveling up the Platte proved to be the real pleasure portion of our long journey, for as we advanced the storms were less frequent until they finally disappeared.

After many days traveling we found ourselves oppossite Fort Laramie for it was located on the south side of the river. Here we saw the first house on our journey after leaving the Morman Cabins this side of where Omaha now is. We tarried here for the noon hour and while we were eating our lunch quite a number of Sioux indians came to us and seated themselves on the ground and commenced to pick the lice from each others heads and crack them between their teeth as though they were precious morsels. This was more filth than I expected to see among human beings and I confess that it was with difficuly that I finished my meal. I have seen thousands of Indians since that day and many of them much lower in the scale of intelligence than these Sioux but I never have witnessed such a scene as that since that day and fondly hope I never will.   After leaving Fort Laramie we entered what was known as the Black hills   They seemed more dark and rugged on the south side of the river than on the north.   The valley on either side was very narrow and sometimes it looked like we were completely hemmed, but by making a sharp curve we would round a hill and start up another narrow valley.   Thus we kept on our way until we were through these hills.

One day my friend Joe and I went out on a hunt and several miles north of the wagon road we found something that resembled the ruins of an ancient castle and quite near it a beautiful spring of clear, cold water bubbling up from the middle of a large flat rock which looked like it had been scooped out on purpose for it. Good water or in fact water at all we found very scarce in that country save in the Platte.

We traveled all day and late in the evening we killed an antelope, but as we were several miles from camp and no moonlight we did not take time to dress it for fear we might be dressed by some wandering Indians or a pack of hungry wolves.   We simply hitched ourselves to it and dragged it to camp.   The meat was excellent and others besides ourselves shared in its goodness and partook of its benefits.   It is only those who travel and camp out in the open air that know what an appetite it gives and how it improves the health.

The fall before we left Illinois I bought a hog, which dressed 150 pounds, for my small family and we ate of it all winter.   When we started west it looked like it had hardly been touched. I told my father that I thought we had meat enough to last us to Oregon and he came to the same conclusion. There was not a single pound of that pig left when we reached Council Bluffs. There we bought more and that was all gone before we reached our destination. If any one wants to improve their health and strength let them travel with wagons and horses and camp out in the open air.

There was one thing that was cheering after we passed into the Black Hills and that was we could leave off cooking with buffalo chips and have plenty of wood. We also found that we were getting into a higher latitude and at times we wanted a better fire than could be made from chips. After passing through these hills we found a large extent of level country again. And as we pressed on, day after day, we eventually came to a stream called Sweetwater and there was a terrible canyon on it known as Devil's Canyon. It was about one and one-half miles in length with solid walls of rock on either side reaching up hundreds of feet. Some of our company who had been to see Chimney Rock concluded, that as this curiosity was near at hand, they would survey its mysteries and see if they were not more beautiful than the Chimney.

Not long after they entered it their feet began to slip on the rocks, worn smooth by the waters. As the waters were rolling and tumbling in terrific majesty and the spray flying in all directions and wetting them, and the roar of the canyon was like mighty thunders, and as they were slipping and falling they wished they had never entered the doleful gorge. However, after a time

It stood and looked at us.—page 14.

they got out alive but bruised and battered, and con-cluded they did not want anything more to do with places named for the devil, that he himself was a very tough customer and if they were much with him they might become like him.

In that same region we found a vast field of ice that the summer suns never melt. By digging down from a foot to two feet through the soil it is found in abund-ance but is said to be poisonous for drinking purposes. The covering to this ice is clothed with a thick carpet of buffalo grass, and when one looks at it they wonder how it is possible for vegetation to grow so near where ice remains all the time, but it does. How far down this ice extends I have no means of knowing as we found no bottom to it.

There is still another curiosity in this region of country. It is that of an immense rock rearing its head up in a seemingly level plain called Indepedence. The name is said to have been given to it by some emi-grants who camped near it on the Fourth of July years before this and celebrated the birthday of our country. The rock is more than a mile in circumference and at least a fourth of a mile in heigth. Unlike Chimney Rock time had not worn its sides away. It was not so smooth, however, but that its ascent could be easily made. And as one climbed its sides he could read hun-dreds of names, and well up into the thousands, for wherever there was room there was a name. Here I saw the names of many whom I had known in my younger days and wondered if they yet lived. This monumental stone made us for the time forget the weariness of our journey.

A friend of mine who crossed the plains in 1852, and whom I always regarded as a truthful man, told me that not far from Independence Rock he went on a hunt one day and in his rambles he found quite a large hill that attracted his notice on account of its peculiar appearance. He approached it and spent some time in its examination and finally with his hatchet that he carried in his belt he chipped off a piece of it and found it to be almost pure lead, and that when he arrived at camp and melted it he saw that it made good bullets, except that it was a little too hard. He brought a piece of it into Oregon and experts pronounced it lead with a small mixture of silver. He never returned to work it and prove its richness.

CHAPTER VII.

The first night after we left Independence Rock we found the grass very scarce near the road and my friend Joe proposed to me that if I would go with him he would take the horses to better feed. We left the train, camped near a small stream and with our rifles and blankets we took the horses about three miles, where finding an excellent lot of grass we proceeded to picket them securely not knowing what might happen during the night.

We were in a valley shaped like a horse shoe with low hills on three sides of it. It was a beautiful spot and covered with luxuriant grass.   When night came we rolled ourselves in our blankets and lay down to sleep, with the heavens above for our tent.   We were up so high on the Rocky Mountains that we did not anticipate much danger from the red men and then we had not kindled a fire that would be a signal that some emigrants were campled there.   We were just getting into a quiet slumber and, of course, not suspecting any danger near, when all of a sudden a mule (which by the way is the best guard one can have on such a journey) raised a terrible snort and instantly every animal was pawing and snorting too, and trying to break loose from their fastenings.   We thought what has happened now to frighten our animals like this and as soon as possible we were up with our guns in hand and among the animals to see if we could find the cause of their fright.   As we came to them we spoke in gentle tones trying to quiet them.   We searched in vain for the cause of their fright but could find none, and finally retired again for the night.

The next morning after daylight we started for our camp with the horses and found that about 150 yards from us a very large grizzly bear had passed during the night.   We were glad the wind blew from him to us and not from us to him for had it been otherwise he would have scented us and have had a royal feast either of human or horse flesh.   The bear must have thought the snort of the horses was thunder at his heels and that he had better be getting away from it as fast as he could, for just opposite where we were at night his bearship showed that he shuffled off with accelerated speed.

As one climbs up the Rocky Mountains he scarcely realizes that he is going up hill the ascent is so gradual. When we at last reached the summit I wondered why they were called Rocky Mountains for there were no rocks in sight, but one vast unbroken plain with here and there a very small amount of timber. When we came to what was known as the Pacific springs and saw the water flowing westward we knew we had came to the place "where gravitation shifting turns the other way." And this we all said is the summit towards which we have all been climbing for weeks and if our decent proves as fortunate as our ascent we will yet land on the Pacific slope all safe and sound for we have had no sickness as yet in all our travels.

From the summit the waters flowed both east and west; pointing toward the rising sun from whence we came and to the setting sun towards which we were journeying. I took my rifle and went out for a little hunt, as much as anything else, I suppose, that I might have it to say in after years that I hunted one day on the summit of the Rocky Mountains or the back bone of our continent. The wind was blowing quite hard and it was very cold so that I did not remain long. In my rambles I did not find either deer, antelope, or rabbit, but I did find a home-made butcher knife with its buck-horn handle, a relic that I prized very highly as it came from the summit. But someone else in the train prized it highly too and appropriated it without leave to his own use, or then I left it by mistake near some of our lonely camp fires.

It was about noon when we passed over the summit

and when we went into camp that night it was cold and frosty although about the 20th of June.   Beyond this we came to the forks of the road, one called Sublet's cut-off and the other the old emigrant road past Fort Bridger.   The cut-off was said to be a little shorter road than the other but a much rougher one.   Here the train separated and we were one among the number who decided to go the Bridger road.   The night we camped near the fort the ice formed at least an inch thick although it was the 1st of July.

After leaving Bridger we passed over a very high ridge and then gradually deceuded into the Bear river country.   When we came near enough to the bottom land to see it fully a sight greeted us that was cheering to both man and beast and seemed to put new life into both.   As far as the eye could reach, for the valley was both wide and long, it was covered with red top from two to four feet high and all our horses had to do as we moved along was to pluck it on either side of the road. Then the only sign of civilization was Fort Bridger a place settled many years before by a man by the name of Bridger from the state of Kentucky.   Now there is said to be beautiful homes and towns all through that country, so that it would be difficult for one of the old emigrants to pass that way and recognize the road over which he then traveled or any of the hills he then passed.

One day when traveling along the borders of this beautiful landscape and through the vast sea of red top we found a creek called Soap creek, which I think was rightly named, for it smelled just like the boiling soft

soap that my mother used to make me stir when I was a
small boy, the scent of which I was not found of, and
which still lingers with me when I think of those days.

CHAPTER VIII.

We knew nothing about the depth of this creek (if
such it could be called) for where it seemed like water
ought to have been was only this soft soapy substance
and very miry.   When we probed it with sticks we found
it was about eighteen inches in depth.   This encouraged
us and we drove in and across without any serious
trouble, only that which we borrowed.   We were afraid,
as the horses' legs were covered with the soap, that it
might be strong enough to eat the hair off and leave
them sore, for there was no water in sight with which
to cleanse them and our wagons.   Nature generally
provides for emergencies, especially if it creates them,
and it was not long until one of the most beautiful
sights of our entire journey greeted us.

We were passing near a great wall of black rock on
our right hand that was several hundred feet in height,
when to our astonishment a great river came gushing
out from beneath it more than a hundred feet wide and
from six inches to three feet in depth   Its waters were
like ice water and of the very best quality, running on
a bed of small gravel and went rushing on towards
Bear river.   Before we reached the opposite shore we
had both our wagons and horses cleansed from the filth
of Soap creek

I looked on that stream without a name with a great

deal of interest and wondered where such a large body
of water came from and how its channel was formed.
The Wind River mountains clad in snow were in full
view and no doubt this stream had its origin there and
that its channel was formed by some great upheaval of
nature.   It was there, and there to stay until some of
nature's convulsions should close it.   Right glad we
were that it did not occur while we were there for we
might have been precipitated through the center of the
earth with Jules Verne, a trip we had no longing for as
we were bound for Oregon so that we might "add fifteen
years to our lives."

Below this a few miles Bear river makes a very sudden
bend like an elbow and goes rushing off towards the
Great Salt Lake.   Near where this bend occurs there is
a curiousity known as Soda Springs.   There are a number of them and some of them excellent soda water.
There is one which deserves special mention called
Steamboat Springs.   There are times when it seems to
be resting and then it is as quiet as a sleeping babe,
when all of a sudden it breaks forth puffing and blowing
like a steamboat and sending its soda sprays far into the
air.   It was sound asleep when we were there and as I
gazed down into its mysterious depths I could but wish
it would wake up and make us emigrants retreat in a
hurry from its commotions.

The country all around these springs bear unmistaka-
ble signs of some mighty shakings and that volcanic fires
were not very far away even then.   A gentleman with
whom I conversed afterwards told me that a number of
them went out on a hunt some ten or twelve miles north

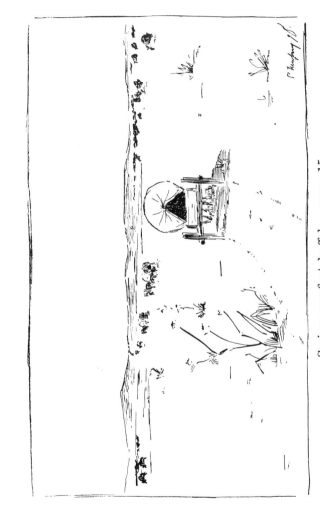

Seeing our first buffalo.—page 15.

of these springs and in their ramblings they came to a depressed valley of small size and in various places over it smoke was coming out of the ground, showing there was fire beneath. The country around the springs and between there and Fort Hall was much better and richer in appearance than thousands of acres over which we had passed beyond Fort Bridger, or even the high plateau on which the fort stands.

It was near these springs that we met all of our old company who had gone the Sublet route, except the old gentleman and his family with whom we had started from Illinois. They got in a hurry and pressed on without any companions save their own and there were seven men and four women of them.

When they had passed Fort Hall and came to a small body of timber some Indians made an attempt to run in ahead of them, and had it not been for the bravery of one women, who had learned to handle a rifle, the Indians would have succeeded. But she with her bravery kept them at a distance until open ground was found, when the Indians retreated to the great joy of the company.

The night after we left the Springs we camped near the foot of a mountain and close to our road there was a large flat rock and near the middle of it a fine soda spring with excellent drinking water came bubbling up. This was the night of the Fourth of July, a day that should never be forgotten by any lover of his country, it matters not in what portion of the world he may be. Here we had a wilderness celebration of the day, as we had quite a large company of our own and besides our own, here I

found my old Illinois friend who was intending to "add
fifteen years to his life." We asked him for a short
speech, which he gave in good style, and then we gave
three cheers for our country, fired our guns, placed our
guards in position and retired for the night. The next
night we camped near Fort Hall, which at the time was
only occupied by some French traders. Uncle Sam's
boys were not there, not even one that we saw, and yet
the fort was among the Sohones or Snake Indians, one
of the worst tribes that ever lived on the American continent for low cunning, meaness and treachery, which
many emigrants found to their sorrow both before and
after this.

Even that year the emigration expected to have protection from the forts, but they were doomed to disap-
pointment, and the savages did as they pleased, roamed
where they liked and stole stock from the poor emigrants,
yet all the time pretending great friendship.

The men at the fort warned us to look out for theiv-
ing Indians and said they would be likely to visit our
camp at night whether we saw anything of them through
the day or not. Sure enough the night we tarried in
full view of the fort they came we supposed about midnight when the guards were being changed and took
three horses and made their escape with them while no
one knew they were gone until the next morning. We
never saw nor heard of then afterwards and knew they
had not strayed from us with their own accord. There
was a Frenchman at the fort who had traveled the road
to western Oregon frequently and he gave us a guide
written in English pointing out the best camping and

watering places which we found afterwards to be of excellent service. The second day's travel from Fort Hall we were overtaken by a Nez Pierce chief and his family, and he asked for the privilege of camping near us as a protection from the Snake Indians. We very gladly consented, for we thought if it was necessary for one Indian to be cautious of others that we had better be on the sharp lookout ourselves. This chief had been educated at the Spaulding mission and could talk the English language very well, at least well enough to be under-stood.

The first night he camped with us the Snakes stole five head of horses from him. In the morning he came and asked for the privilege of his family camping near us while he went out in search of the stolen horses. This chief had been beyond the fort buying emigrant stock and recuiting them so that they could travel to his home at the Mission. He was gone five days and we all expected that he was murdered but one evening about sun-down he came up with our camp, bringing all the stolen animals. During his absence his companions did not show any uneasiness for fear he might never return. He was not hurt himself in the least, while he declared that he killed all three of the Indians who had done the stealing. He traveled with us about two weeks and then left for his home. Before he left he tried very hard to get me and my family to go home with him and teach his people how to read and write and farm and cook, promising us a good home with a good house and orchard with all the land I wanted and plenty of horses and cattle. We declined his generous offer for we felt

we had been among Indian tribes as long as we cared
about. I learned afterward from those who knew him
that he would have been as punctual to his promises as
any white man.

Below Fort Hall were the American Falls, one road
to Oregon crossed the river near them while the other
continued on the south side. We traveled on the south
side of Snake river and it was not long until we encountered a very hilly and rocky country, making it hard on
our wagons and teams and very trying on our patience.
It was very difficult to travel over them and still more
difficult to find plenty of grass for our horses.

When we came to Goose creek we found that the road
to California went up that stream and here quite a number of our train left us for the Golden State whom we
never saw again and among that number was my friend
Joe.   There were times when we had to travel so near
the water that it seemed like our wagons would upset
and land us all in a watery grave.   On the upper side
was a rocky wall and we could not dodge sometimes six
inches without great danger.   Finally we arrived at a
small level spot with some grass on it and halted for the
noon hour.   After the meal, while we were waiting for
our horses to feed, one gentleman approached another
and said:

"I do not see what this part of the world was made
for.   It certainly is of no use whatever."

"You are a very foolish man." said the other, "there
would be a tremendous hole in the world were it not for
this country that you regard as worthless, and you might
have to travel several hundred miles to get around it,

but now you can get over it by going a few miles, bump-a-ta-bump over the rocks. I perfer it just as it is for my part without any amendments."

One day while traveling on the south side of the river we encountered immense swarms of black nats and mosquitoes and it was very difficult to tell which bit the worst. Sometimes we thought it was one and then we would conclude it must be the other. One thing sure they both bit until our faces were so swollen we could scarcely see. That night we camped on the river bottom and after we had begun to eat, a small cloud came floating by with a slight sprinkle of rain and a very sudden gust of wind. In a moment after this all passed by, our gnats and mosquitoes were gone to some other country, "seeking whom they might devour" there. But, horrible to relate, we looked at our victuals, for the wind came on so suddenly we had no time to cover them, and they were filled with gray sand until it was difficult to tell what they were. We did not dare to throw them away for there was no chance to purchase any more so we cleansed them as best we could and ate them while the sand gritted between our teeth.

The country below this began to show signs of improvement, the hills were lower and not so rocky and the grass was more abundant. With the improved country there began to be more fresh Indian signs and by consulting our guide paper it told us to look out for the treacherous Snakes. One night we camped on Salmon creek where there was excellent grass. When night began to approach we found, as the creek here formed a horse shoe in shape, that we could

put our wagons across the open part of the shoe and our
horses between them and the creek and station a strong
guard at the ford, which was at the extreme bend of the
shoe and the only place where an Indian could take a
horse over the stream, that we would be comparatively
safe.   After this was all done and darkness came on we
heard what we at first thought were wolves, first on one
hill top and then on another, but as we had not seen a
wolf for several hundred miles we concluded it was
the Indians giving the signal that it was a good night to
do some stealing from the emigrants.   We placed out a
strong guard, changing it at midnight, placeing one
man at the ford of the creek.   The next morning the
best animal in the train was missing and when we came
to examine the ford the horse tracks were plainly seen.
The men who kept guard at the ford were called and the
one who stood guard the first part of the night said all
was right when he retired, while the one who guarded
the after part of the night said he got tired guarding the
ford and concluded there was no danger and went and
lay down by his own animal.   He acknowledged that he
saw a horse cross the stream but no one was leading it
and it would soon be found.   The opposite side was examined and soon a moccasin track was seen and also the
place where he had mounted the animal and left for
parts unknown.   A council was immediately called and
some of the men were breathing out threatenings against
the man who said he saw the horse cross the ford, for
his own acknowledgement showed him a miserable coward.   Instead of guarding where he was placed he went
away some distance leaving the ford exposed, which was

the important place to be guarded. Some wanted to expell him from the company, while others thought if he was expelled the Indians would soon dispatch him.

CHAPTER X.

The question to be settled was, shall we let the Indian keep the horse or shall we try to find it and take it from him? The conclusion was to let the train remain in camp at least a few hours and some men go out in search of the stolen animal. The next question was, who will go? Volunteers were called for. The owner of the stolen animal said he would go for one. I said I would go, and then three more volunteerad, making a company of five. But among the volunteers the one who failed to guard the ford was not one of them for he prefered evidently to stay where there was more company. Enough had to be left to guard the women and children and horses and see that no more mischief was done while we were gone.

In the company which went out to search was one young man from the state of Maine with whom I had become quite intimate by acquaintance, as we had often stood guard together and conversed on various subjects and occasionally on the subject of religion. I had often urged him to be prepared for the world to come as none of us knew at what moment an Indian might put a ball or an arrow through us. He swore he was not afraid of all the red skins from the Missouri river to the Willamette valley, and that if they killed him he would be safe anyway, for all men were sure at least to be saved. He seemed very strong in that belief and I asked him if he did not think he would weaken if he thought he was going to die.

"Oh, no, sir, you will not find me such a coward as that when the test comes."

That morning the searching party ate a very light breakfast and were soon off on the chase and as we did not expect to be gone long we did not take even a canteen of water with us. After crossing the creek we only went a short distance until we found where the Indian with his stolen property commenced ascending a hill. We followed on and soon found that in order to ascend the steep hill the Indian had gone up that we must travel zig-zag as he had done. We did this and yet it seemed as though we would never get to the summit, but after awhile we found that we were at the top of the hill and here we halted for a breathing spell. The view from the summit was a grand one, grander than I can describe. North of us as well as south of us were mountains piled on mountains, until they reached into the clouds, covered with timber. East of us we could trace the serpentine course of Snake river as well as west of us. At the foot of the hill and near the confluence of Salmon creek with Snake river our tents and wagons could be plainly seen glistering in the morning sun. We found we were on a very high ridge and that the tracks of the stolen animal were still pressing southward. All the time we were looking in all directions for the Indian.

The morning was all that heart could wish save it was a little warm. Every thing about us, even the fresh

Chased by buffalos.—page 15.

tracks of the horse that was stolen, seemed to indicate
that we were going to be successful in the chase.   Our
hopes were firm and buoyant and seemed to float high
above all obstacles.   Three of us then were young men
not more than twenty-three or four years of age and the
other two about thirty-five or forty.   We followed on up
this divide until we came to a place where the Indian
had halted and cooked his breakfast.   After an examination we found the fire was still burning slowly and
this led us to believe we were getting very near him.
While we halted at this fire the dusky thief came in
sight, not more than a half mile from us.   This ani-
mated greatly the three youngest of us and away we
went as fast as our horses could run.   The two older
ones were more cautious and called out to us, "boys,
look out and do not venture too far ahead."   We
had a hard chase for a mile or two and at last Indian
and horse both disappeared, but the tracks were plainly
to be seen.   The young man from Maine was the leader.
Finally we came to another canyon coming into that of
Salmon creek at right angles and as we turned up the
west canyon, still following the tracks, our leader said,
"here are the tracks, boys."   Just then there was the
report of a rifle and he exclaimed, "I am killed!"

CHAPTER XI.

I heard the report of a rifle and for a moment supposed
that he had shot at an Indian, but when I looked for the
smoke from the gun I saw it was near a large rock and
some distance below us.   He was still on his horse,

holding his rifle, when he called out he was shot and killed. We asked him to go towards camp and we would try to secure the Indian. We dismounted and went near the edge of the canyon trying to get a shot at the Indian who had wounded our fellow traveler. There was no human being in sight anywhere, save an Indian on horseback galloping off towards the mountains to the south. We were satisfied he was not the one who had done the mischief, for there was not time enough since the report of the rifle.

Our friend managed to get about 200 yards towards camp and got off at the foot of a hill and after dismounting he fell over and we supposed he was dead. Our search for the Indian having proved fruitless we directed our steps toward the wounded man. Just as we came up where he was the two men we had left behind came riding up. He was bleeding profusely and we hastened to remove his clothing and make an examination. We soon found the ball had entered the body on the right side between the two first ribs and had passed entirely through, coming out between the same ribs on the opposite side. We turned him on his back and the blood would spurt out some distance from the body and then we would turn him over when it would do the same. We at once decided that one man should go to camp, some twelve miles distant, and give the alarm and secure help. He made the trip in safety and when he arrived there was intense excitement and many wondered whether we would not all be killed. From the time the help left the camp until their return were hours of gloom and many wished we had let the Indian keep the horse without any effort on our part and have traveled on our westward journey.   We could better things immensely sometimes if we could see ahead as far as we can see back after the deed is done.

After our messenger had left for camp the wounded man began to call for water, declaring he must have it or he would soon be dead.   To add to his greater misery the sun poured down its heat with terrible force and we had no means of shelter.   Not a bunch of willows or a patch of brush any where near us out of which we could construct a shade.   The question was: how can we obtain water?   When we left camp we only expected to be gone a short time and did not take our canteens.   We commenced then to examine our boots and out of all of them there was only one of mine found without holes. I soon pulled it off and Mr. Strong, the owner of the stolen animal, started to find water.   This only left two of us to care for the one in distress, and the one left with me said he could not stand the sight of blood and went off so far that he knew an Indian could not reach him either with a rifle ball or an arrow.   I tried to get him to go to the top of the hill at the foot of which we were located and stand guard, but no, he was not willing to go there and watch.

While he was absent and the other gone for water, Mr. H. said, "pray for me Parson, I am afraid I am going to die and if I do I am a lost man."

Said I, "why pray for you if everybody is going to be saved."

With a deep tone of anguish in his voice he called out. "Do pray for me.   Universalism will do to live with but

I find it will not do to die with. Oh, my dear friend, pray for me before I am gone for I cannot live much longer."

I turned my face towards the top of the hill and with eyes wide open and watching for Indians (for I expected every moment we would be shot) I prayed for him as best I could.

After the prayer closed, he cried out, "Oh, Mother, Mother, I want to see you."

Said I, "your Mother is in the State of Maine."

"Then," said he, "let me see my brother's wife before I die."

"You shall, if you will only live a few hours and we can get you where she is."

He said, with a deep pleading look in his eyes, "Parson, you had better leave me, for I am bound to die and you have a family to care for and I have none."

"My friend," said I, "as long as their is breath in your body I will not leave you, for if we must perish we will perish side by side."

The idea of intense thirst again seized him and he said, "Will that man never come with water? Oh, water, water, or I die."

After awhile Mr. Strong returned and told us that he went down into the canyon about 500 feet with great difficulty, when he came to a square offset of at least 500 feet more and came near plunging headlong over the precipice and that if it had not been for a small bush he would have made the fatal plunge. But he made his way out and to us in safety.

"What shall we do," said he, "if he does not have

water soon he will be dead."

In the forenoon, as we rounded the elbow of the canyon, I had noticed an Indian trail leading down towards
camp and I thought he might possibly find water by
following it. He went and returned after a little while
with hardly a half boot full of water, as it had leaked
out. The wounded man drank heartily of it but it made
him sick and he commenced to vomit, and the blood to
spurt from both sides of his body. Fearing he would
bleed to death we bandaged him with some pocket hand-
kerchiefs, when, almost instantly he went into spasms
and we had to remove them. I got one sup of water
from the first that was brought in the boot that I had
worn from the states and I really (as inconsistent as it
may seem) thought it was the best water I had ever
tasted. Water was brought the second time and it
seemed to greatly relieve the sufferer.

CHAPTER XII.

It was about noon when our messenger started for
camp, and, as he had to travel twenty or twenty-five
miles on a poor animal, we knew he would not return
with the help until it would be very late in the afternoon, if not night. After consulting about the matter
we concluded we had better start for camp and meet
them on the way, as the flow of blood had almost ceased
and he seemed much easier. Late in the afternoon we
lashed our guns to my Indian pony, which was to be
led, together with the wounded man's horse, by one
man, while the other man led the horse on which Mr. H.

rode and I got on behind him so as to hold him in the saddle, as it was an American one without any horn that he could hold to. I had neither stirrups nor a blanket and I did not dare to let go my hold of him for fear he would fall from the horse. I rode that entire distance without dismounting or even relaxing my hold on him for a single moment. We concluded as the safest plan to follow an Indian trail as it was likely to pass over the best and easiest route. In places the trail was very rocky and every time the animal would make a blunder, and that was quite frequently, he would call out or then groan, it seemed to me as loud as he could, and I would beg him to remain quiet if possible for fear the Indians might hear the noise and attack us and we could not defend ourselves as all our fire arms were fast. We had not gone half the distance to camp when night overtook us with nothing but starlight and it very dark. We missed the help sent out for us and made our way as best we could over hills and around them and through dark canyons one after another. At last when we began to be very tired and wondering if we were not lost, Mr. Strong called out, "here is our camp just ahead of us. I see the lights." We arrived about 11 o'clock, tired, anxious and hungry, not having a mouthful to eat since early in the morning. I never entered any place with a more thankful heart in my life than I did my tent in the wilderness that night. Thankful that none of our party had been killed and that although I was in a few feet of Mr. H. when the Indian shot him, yet the ball did not penetrate my body.

When those who went out to meet us found we were

gone and they had not found us by the way, they concluded, as they still had some daylight to spare, that they would follow the tracks of the stolen animal and find the place where the Indian had done the shooting. They went up the west canyon some distance above where we had gone and found a trail with the tracks of a shod horse leading down into it, and soon found a large, natural barn, large enough to hold at least, so they thought, forty head of horses. Here he had fastened the animal and went out some distance above until he came to another rock with a hole in it large enough for a rifle and to take sight and there he fired what he thought was a deadly shot. Why he did not remain behind his fort and continue to shoot the rest of us we never knew. It was about 2 o'clock in the morning when they returned. We were all glad to be together once more, even with the sore experience of the day.

The day we were out on the hunt for the stolen horse an ox train came along late in the afternoon and an old gentleman and his partner, the one who had failed to guard the ford, concluded they would go with them and wait next morning for our arrival. That night the Indians stole one of their horses and they had to remain where they were as the ox train had no special interest in them and they expected us along soon. They waited until near noon, when the one who had stood such poor guard came back to see what had become of us and to procure help to bring his partner and wagon to us. After he had been gone some time and the old gentleman left alone to guard his property, mad at the Indians and chaffing under his loss, resolved that he would kill the

River issuing from a wall of solid rock.—page 26.

first Indian he saw. They were camped near Salmon
Falls and he soon saw an Indian seat himself on a rock
and commence to spear the Salmon which were then
running up the river. He placed himself behind a rock,
leveled his gun at the Indian's breast and fired, killing
him instantly as he tumbled into the river. Then it was
that he began to think very seriously over what he had
done, and as a "guilty conscience needs no accuser," he
became very uneasy and greatly alarmed for fear other
Indians might have seen one of their fellows slain. He
finally concluded the best plain was to get out of there
as speedily as possible. He hitched up old gray (his
remaining horse) and then placed himself on the other
side of the wagon tongue and he and gray pulled the
wagon up quite a hill towards our camp, when his partner met him and brought him safely in.

We remained in camp three days so as to relieve the
wounded man as much as possible. He improved all
the time but was very sore and hard on that account to
handle. The third day we fixed a swinging cot to the
bows of a spring wagon and the fourth morning we
placed him in it, hitched up our teams and journeyed
on, for we were afraid that something as bad as bullets
might overtake us. There were no stations by the way
that furnished provisons to hungry emigrants and we
were all liable to starve to death if we delayed too long.
The young man improved steadily but the swinging of
the cot and the jolting of the wagon brought many a
hearty grunt or groan from him. When we reached the
Cascade Mountains he seemed as well as ever and I never
heard him swear but once, and then he turned to me

with an apology.

I remember once being sent for to visit a man who was thought to be dying and he said:

"Oh, Parson, if I ever get over this I will be a better man."

"If you get over it," I said "you will forget this promise and be as bad or worse than before."

He got over it and went to keeping saloon and I concluded he was not bettering much.

Having spoken of what become of the wounded man and how he prospered, I will now return to the thread of my story. After we left our camp at Salmon Creek the scenes and intense excitement of the past week began gradually to subside. Everything moved along smoothly without any more interruptions from the Indians, but we were by no means asleep and heedless of our danger and that we were still in an enemy's country. But before I speak further of our onward march I want to relate a scene which transpired on the north side of Snake river, about fifty miles above Fort Boise, the place where Boise City, the capitol of Idaho, is now located. Here occured one of the most brutal mascacres that ever took place on the American continent. I do not mean in the great number killed but the manner in which the fiends accomplished their purpose. It was so inhuman that no writer or historian ever dared to tell how it was done and had it not been for those who came on after them it never would have been told.

An emigrant train was moving along quitely, not suspecting that any danger was near, when all of a sudden the savage yell was heard, striking terror to every heart, and well it might, for out of the entire company only two boys were left as survivors of the scene of that day. Heaven looked down in pity on this company as the dying groans of the sufferers ascended. To fully accomlish their brutal work they burned the wagons, and then used the iron rods to burn their victims into insensibility. The two lads who were saved, one, I think, was about twelve years old and the other fourteen. When the work of death begun the youngest boy stole away and hid in some tall grass some distance from the scene. The other lad was pierced through the body with an arrow, and, it is supposed, the Indians left him for dead.

After the Indians had accomplished their deadly work and had taken the stock and left the scene, the smaller boy heard the sound of a passing horse and very cautiously raising himself he peeped out from his hiding place, when to his joy he saw that it was a white man. He immediately ran to him and was lifted up behind him and carried to a place of safety. When this lone rider saw what had been done he passed the scene in a hurry and did not see the boy with the arrow in his body. After awhile the one pierced with an arrow came to himself, although somewhat dazed, and found that he could travel and made his way to Fort Boise fifty miles distant, where an English surgeon, who had examined him, found that the arrow was showing itself on both sides of his body. He extracted it and took care of him until he was able to travel and then sent him on to Oregon.

Joe Lane, who, I believe was then the Territorial Governor of Oregon, made the lad a present of a thousand dollars, so as to assist him in getting an education. When I saw him a year or two after this he seemed well and strong. I understood that he and his brother vowed vengeance on the Snake Indians and determined to kill every one they could. But whether they ever went into that country again I never learned.

Now I must ask the privilege of returning the second time to my story and will try to stick to it a little closer than I have done during the first of this chapter. We had two brothers with us who failed to agree very well with our captain and they concluded to travel and camp alone, but it was very plainly to be seen they had no intention of getting far from us for fear they might get into trouble with the Indians. They traveled and camped near us for some time but no difficulty occured to mar either their or our peace.

When we arrived on the summit overlooking the Malheur river we saw in the valley a large circular fire and the Indians killing and eating grasshoppers and crickets for supper, but as we did not relish that kind of "grub" we did not apply for any; in fact it was only a few moments after they saw us until the fires were all out and not an Indian to be seen. Naturally, when Indians were so wild they would not visit our camp, we thought they meant mischief. We camped below the ford of the river and the two brothers camped still lower down. Just at dark we heard the sound of wolves again; just such a sound as we heard the night before Mr. H. was shot on Salmon creek, and we knew that we must be cautious again. We stationed guards in our part of the

company and one of the brothers stood guard for them.
Along towards midnight the sharp report of a rifle was
heard and the whole camp was aroused from their slum-
bers. An Indian had sneaked to our portion of the
camp and had stolen our best horse, and by some means
had passed our guard and was trying to pass the guard
of the other camp. The lower guard called to the horse,
as he saw him moving off, "whoa, there! whoa there!"
Instead of stopping, the animal went faster and this
caused the Indian to straighten himself on the horse.
As he did so the guard fired and the Indian concluded
it was rather close range and jumped from the horse and
went down an embankment at least twenty feet. The
next morning we saw where he had made his leap, but
there was no sign of blood, but his tracks showed plain
enough that he left there in a great hurry.

On the bank of this stream, and not far from the
crossing, were two springs not more than three feet
apart. One was nice, cold water to drink and the other
would scorch a bucksin cracker in a second.

The bottom land on this river seemed to be very good,
but where timber could be got for fencing and firewood
is more than I could tell, for there was none nearer than
the mountains and they were a great many miles away.

Not many days after leaving the Malheur river, five
young men of our company concluded we were not
traveling fast enough to suit them, as they seemed in a
great hurry to reach western Oregon. They went to
Snake river and bought a canoe of the Indians, for we
were then in the borders of another tribe who were
friendly, and three of them with the larger share of their

baggage got in the vessel and started down toward the
Columbia river, while the other two took the horses and
followed the emigrant road. One of those who went
in the canoe had been very sick on the journey and I had
taken him in and hauled him more than 200 miles, while
I went afoot, and the bargain was that I should have his
horse to work with mine over the ranges of mountains
we had yet to pass, so that my family would not have to
walk. When he was about to start for the river that
morning I kindly, but very firmly, reminded him of his
bargain and told him I thought he was doing me and my
family a great injustice, when we had helped him during his sickness. He acknowledged his contract with
me in the presence of Mr. Strong of Michigan, but said
"I am determined to go and take my horse with me."
Mr. S. said, "Parson if he can prosper in doing wrong
let him go and I will see you safe into the Willamette
valley." This is the same man who failed to stand guard
at the ford of Salmon creek and was virtually the cause
of Mr. H. being shot. When the two men who had gone
on with the horses arrived at the ford of the Deschutes
river they heard that the bodies of three white men had
been found at the mouth and when they investigated
they found them to be the bodies of their three companions who had attempted the navigation of strange streams
to them. Before we reached Burnt river I found so far
as I was concerned there was another very serious trouble
ahead. We were without meat and had very little flour
left. None in our train had any provisions to spare but
expected they would have to buy for themselves. My
friend, who had promised to see me safe through, said,

"Parson, I will divide with you as long as I can if you cannot buy any." I told him if he would lend me some money, for I had spent all mine crossing some ferries, that I would go ahead and see if provisions could not be bought of other emigrant trains. It so happened that on that same day I heard of a Baptist minister who had some meat to sell.

In traveling on we found him camped not far from the road down towards the river. When I approached him I told what I wanted and his reply was, "you can have what you wish." I asked the price and he said he thought it ought to be worth ten cents a pound, as that was what he paid for it in Indiana, and after hauling it that far he ought to have as much as that. He could not and would not be hard on poor emigrants like himself. I bought what I thought would last beyond the Cascade Mountains into civilization and several others did the same.

After we all arrived in Oregon I formed his acquaintance again and found him a consistent christian gentleman. His name was Chandler and he was the only man I ever talked with who did not travel more than one sabbath on the plains, and on that one he broke his wagon pole. One reason why meat was so scarce was that we had not seen a deer or an antelope for hundreds of miles and we concluded if there was any they must be about the mountains.

We crossed Burnt river and ascended the divide between it and Powder river, passing not far from where Baker city now stands, not thinking once that there were immense fortunes in gold in the earth over which

He exclaimed, "I am killed!"—page 38.

we were then traveling. From Powder river we passed
over another divide between it and Grande Rounde
valley and when we advanced far enough to behold the
valley I thought it was the most beautiful spot I had
ever seen anywhere. Its average width is said to be
twenty miles and its length forty. We crossed near the
upper portion of the valley and near where the town of
Union now stands. As far as we could see down the
valley it was one immense field of red top, as also to the
mountains above us.

Indians sometimes manifest a great deal of shrewdness
in money-making schemes as well as white folks. While
camped in Grande Rounde valley a Cayuse Indian came
to us and said he had viewed out and worked a road
leading up the Blue Mountains (which lay on the west
side of the valley) and that it was much better than the
old road and that for fifty cents a wagon he would pilot
us through. Some went with him, but from what those
said who went the old road, there was but little, if any.
improvement. It was not very far across and I think
as good a mountain road as I ever traveled. After passing over the mountain we found a high rolling prarie
country with but little timber but good grass in abundance.

We finally came to the Umatilla river near where the
town of Pendleton now is and camped for the night.
Before we had unharnessed our teams a Cayuse Indian
came riding up on a very fine American animal and invited me to get on behind him and he would show me a
better camping place. I told him to come up to the
wagon wheel so I could get on. When he came he pre-

sented the wrong side of the horse to me.   I told him
to turn round and when I mounted the horse he laughed
heartily and said, "this man squaw, this man squaw."
It is a fact that an Indian gets on his horse on the opposite side from the American and that the American gets
up on the same side a squaw does, and this was the
reason why he called me "squaw."   We rode up the
river quite a little distance and he showed me a most
beautiful place to camp where there was an abundance
of grass.   When we returned they had unharnessed and
we tarried for the night.

CHAPTER XIII.

The day we left the Umatilla river there was an ox
train behind us, perhaps three-quarters of a mile, and
they stampeded in spite of their drivers.   We heard
them coming just in time to give the road for they would
have ran over everything in their way.   Their wagons
only missed ours a few inches and they passed without
doing us any harm.   No cause was ever known for this
runaway for they had not been frightened in the least.
When their drivers wanted them to travel up lively after
this they had to use their whips very often.   The oxen
were very poor and one would think they could not be
whipped into a run, but they did run about four miles
and then halted of their own accord as though nothing
had happened.   In all the stampedes with oxen I ever
knew of they always kept the road and nothing, it would
seem, could induce them to leave it.   This day we ate
our last mouthful of bread, but I found two batchelors

who had plenty of crackers and bought what I thought would do us until we reached our destination.

We crossed the John Day river without any trouble, but when we came to the Deschutes they wanted an extravagant price for taking us over on the ferry. A Cayuse Indian came along and proposed to take all our horses across for a dollar. When the ferryman found that the Indian had contracted with us for the horses, he concluded he would take us over, men, women, children and wagons for a dollar a wagon. The Indian examined all the horses very carefully and finally selected an Indian pony of mine to ride. He told us, when he rode into the river, to start the horses after him and he would land them all safely on the other side. He started and very soon found his horse had to swim, when he dropped from its back and caught it by the tail, the horse striking out at quite a lively gait for the opposite shore. All the others followed and every one was safely landed as the Cayuse had promised. One thing was very evident, that the pony had been accustomed to such work for it did the job so easy and in a kind of matter-of-fact way.

It was at the mouth of this river that the bodies of the three unfortunate young men were found who attempted to navigate treacherous waters with a small vessel.

After crossing we did not have to go far until we came to Willow creek and those who intended traveling over the mountains instead of going by the Dalles must follow up this stream. Those who had money concluded to go by the Dalles, for on this route they had to pay the boats running on the Columbia river, while those without means decided to go the mountain road which meant "without money and without price." Here, of course, our ways parted and after we had said a kind farewell to each other, those who were bound for the mountains turned to the left up the creek named above and soon found excellent bunch grass for their teams and willows for fire wood. We heard that the mountain road was a very hard one to travel, but a little roughness, and, in fact, a great deal, had no terrors any more for us for we had become accustomed to such things. It was said to be eighty miles across with but little work on the road. On the east side the ascent was quite gradual and there was real romance in climbing, especially after we came to tall timber where the echo sounded so loudly. One lady in the company, with a very strong voice, then commenced to sing, "when up the mountain climbing we will sing this merry strain." It seemed to do all hands good to hear the voice of song in the wild woods, as but few had felt like singing for a thousand miles back.

After we came to the tall timber we had enough to try the patience of the most patient. Large rocks were in the road and the storms had blown the trees across them and we had to frequently use handspikes and raise our wagons over them, go a few rods and then do the same work over. All the way over was not so bad as that I have just described, but sometimes we would travel several miles without much hindrance This road had been view out by Messrs. Barlow, Carver and Rector. Once they were lost and had to subsist on long, slimy snails for some time. Mr. Rector used to own and operate a flour mill on Mark West creek, a few miles above Santa Rosa, and a short distance above the road leading from Santa Rosa to Healdsburg. The property is now used as a sanitarium.

When fully into the mountains we found that some one was traveling on before us who had not lost the fun that was in him. Every now and then he would blaze a tree (and take tar from his wagon) and write thereon "left her rip at such an hour and day." We kept seeing this sign frequently as we traveled on up the mountain over logs and rocks. Finally we got up about the summit where we saw the end gate of a wagon standing and the very significant sign placed on it, "couldn't rip any longer, couldn't," and we looked around and there was his wagon completely demolished by "ripping," as he called it, over the rock and logs so much. I often wished afterwards that I could find the man who wrote those signs for I thought there must be something extra in him when he could have the wear and tear of more than 2000 miles travel and still retain so much good nature. The signs left by this man made us all feel better and assisted us in over-coming the difficulties by the way.

We camped one night near the foot of Mount Hood, in a small prairie, and found good water, poor grass and a cold frosty night, even if it was about the middle of August. There was some improvements in the road from this place but still we had to pass over many a rock and log after this. We finally came to the place of all places, so far as a name was concerned, we had already,

many miles back, passed the Devil's canyon, and now to
think after the long tidious journey of the plains and
before we could reach the home we had in view, we had
actually to go over the Devil's Back Bone. It almost
made us shudder although we had been used to hard
names and hard roads. When we got on to it (that is
the Devil's Back Bone) we found the best road in all
the mountain we had yet passed over and concluded
there was not much in a name after all, although some
people think there is a great deal. It was a long divide
between two streams, but very narrow, with just room
for wagons and teams to pass. On either side there was
immense canyons so far down that we could not see
where they terminated. The sight was a grand one, but
the road you must keep or plunge headlong with self,
family, wagon and team down, down towards the regions
below. I was really glad when we were safely over it,
but why rejoice at this when greater trouble by far was
just ahead of us a few miles.

CHAPTER XVI.

We had been told by some men who had been over
these mountains before that there was one hill to go
down and that we must fasten a tree to the wagon for
safety. We approached it with fear resting on our
minds but with a firm determination that "what man
has done, man can do." When we came in sight of it
I confess it was very forbidden as it seemed almost as
straight up and down as the walls of a house. My wife
tried to ride down it in the wagon with our two children

but became alarmed for fear the wagon would go end
over end, so I halted and helped her and the children
out. Then she started with them to decend the hill one
in her arms and holding the other by the hand, when
she found that it was going to endanger their lives as
well as her own and she called out "I cannot go another
step without help."

It was impossibe for me at the time to render any assistance as I had all I could do to manage the team. I
had fastened two logs to the hind axle, each about fourteen feet long, and then locked both hind wheels. These
logs were about eight inches through and I found it very
difficult to keep my feet and manage the horses. After
a travel down hill of more than a mile and a half I found
myself at the foot and drove the team out of the road,
hitched them and commenced to ascend. I would go a
little distance and then blow, and then a little farther
and puff, and after an absence of almost two hours I
came in sight of my family all seated on the same rock
they occupied when I left them. We commenced the
decent and after many hard struggles we managed to
get to our wagon again very thankful and had no broken
bones to mend and no other hill as bad as this one to go
down.

The streams in the Cascade Mountains run very
swiftly and we found their depths very deceiving. We
crossed one named Zigzag several times and the first
time we crossed it looked like it might be ten inches or a
foot in depth, and when we drove into it we found it
was at least two feet deep. Some came very near being
drowned at the first crossing and were very willing after

An Indian arrow pierced his body.—page 48.

this to get into the wagon.   There were times when it
was even difficult for the horses to keep on their feet
and at the same time pull the wagon across.   The rocks
over which the waters ran so swiftly were worn as
smooth as glass and this added to the burden of the
team.   We had five days of this rough mountain travel
but without a single accident, even if we did have to
travel over the Devil's Back Bone and down the worst
hill that a wagon and team ever went hitched together.
I have heard other emigrants tell about letting their
wagons down hill by ropes, but the horses or cattle were
led without the wagon.   After crossing Zigzag for the
last time we found, not far away, a little grass by the
side of a small stream and concluded we would camp for
the night.   Gladly, we thought, this is our last night in
these mountains and our main troubles will soon be at
an end.

We arose very early for we knew from the description
which had been given us that we still had between fifteen
and twenty miles to go that day, which was the twenty-
second day of August, 1851.   When we came to breakfast we found that we had enough crackers for our
children through the day by being very saving of them
and that so far as we were concerned we must make that
twenty miles on one cracker and a cup of coffee.   We
ate it and started with a courage which knew no such
word as fail.   We thought it very poor policy to give up
when we were almost in sight of final victory and yet we
knew it would be very hard work to travel all day on
such a light breakfast.   On and on we went over hills
and hollows as fast as our poor team could take us.   It

was real nice to see the mountains beginning to flatten out and our road improving greatly in smoothness. We knew from the appearance of the country that we were nearing Foster's at the foot of the mountain.

No one knows what gladness fills the soul when after traveling and toiling as long as we had, and the last day on empty stomachs, they begin to see and know that they would soon be there. Such joy cannot be described and only those know of it who have passed through such scenes. For one I felt like saying, "hip, hip, hurrah." But if I had been disposed to exult and feel proud of our success, pride would have had a great tumble in a moment's time when I thought, "here I am 2000 miles and more from home with a family to feed and nothing to feed them on and no money to buy anything with but three bits and that borrowed."

It is said that a peacock struts most beautifully until his eyes happen to light on his ugly feet then all his feathers fall in a moment's time. Had I been disposed to feel proud when I thought of my slim purse and our poor clothing pride would have instantly fled.

Finally we drove up in front of a log cabin where signs of plenty could be seen.

PART SECOND.

CHAPTER XVII.

At the foot of the Cascade Mountains I propose to begin my experiences of western life, for here I had my first struggle. When we drove up in front of Mr. Foster's house a gentleman came out to the front gate and I asked him if his name was Foster. He said it was. Walking up near him I said:

"We are here and almost starved, having traveled all day on one cracker and some coffee, and now, sir, if you will supply our wants I will give you the last cent of money I have in the world, which is three bits, and to-morrow I will work for you until you say you are fully paid."

He replied that a great many of the emigrants who had passed there had abused him and called him Old Picayune Foster. "Now, sir, if you will speak a kind word for me as you go up the valley I will let you have what you want for the money you have without the work."

I told him I certainly would do that much and thanked him very gratefully besides. He had killed a fine, fat three-year-old beef the day before and he gave me at least ten pounds of that and a nice lot of flour and said: "There is the hoe and yonder is the potato patch, help yourself. I will go to the barn and throw some hay down for your horses for there is no grass near here."

I will leave the reader to guess the amount of supper we ate, and we afterward slept soundly all night. Often in talking with men who had passed Mr. Foster's, both before and after we did, I heard them abuse him, and when I would tell of his kindness to us it would astonish them to think he had been so liberal. I never knew why he treated us so kindly, but one thing I can say, I was glad to find a friend when we really wanted one for we were strangers in a strange land.

The next morning I went to him again and thanked him and asked him if he could tell me where I could get some work to do. He said he thought a man about a mile from him, and directly on our road, wanted help for he had just thrashed his grain with an old chaff piler and now he wanted to clean it with a fanning mill. We found the man and the place and the work and soon a bargain was made and he was to board us, if my wife would do the cooking, and give me a dollar and a half a day.

We remained with him two days and then traveled on up the valley in search of work and a home. Emigrants that year were allowed, if they were married, 320 acres of land and as we traveled on we made inquiry where homes could be found. We came to a stream called Mollala and crossed it on the main mail route up the country from Oregon city. It was a beautiful stream of pure mountain water and we camped there and found grass in abundance.

There was a man living near the ford who had been there a number of years, being among the first to go to Oregon overland. He seemed to be a nice quiet gentleman. He had married prior to 1850 a very worthy young lady, and all who married before that date were entitled to 640 acres. This he had secured from the best land in the territory, for Oregon was not then a state. He kept a Post Office at his place and one day in his absence the mail came and his wife opened the sack and among other letters she found one directed to her husband in a women's hand writing. Curiousity prompted her to open it and she found that it was a letter from his wife in the states, stating that her team was about to give out and she wished he would come and meet her and help her in to the Willamette valley. When he returned his wife showed him the letter and he acknowledged all, but had quietly kept it from her.

"What had I better do," said he, "I do not want any trouble with you women, for I have deceived both of you."

"You must go and meet her and help her over the mountains, then bring her here and we will settle the matter without any trouble whatever," she exclaimed.

He went and met his first wife and brought her to his home and said to the women:

"I do not want any law suit or scandal about this. You two talk it over and decide between yourselves and the one that will live with me I will live with her and the other one I will give 320 acres of land and build a house and barn on it at my own expense and furnish some stock for it," mentioning the amount.

The first one spoke up immediately and said to the other lady, "you have lived with him a great deal longer than I have and you can continue to do so."

He went to work and soon erected buildings and moved her on to the property and after awhile she married and they both lived there side by side as peacable as lambs. This story was told to me by a man who was intimately acquainted with all the parties and from what I knew of him I think he told the truth. Of course, this was something unusal, more especially the latter portion of it where they came to such an agreeable understanding and lived peacably for years close together. The other part, which told of the man marrying one women in the states and then another in Oregon, was nothing uncommon, for it had been done before this, and it has been done many times since.

The next stream we came to was called Abiqua and a man by the name of Allen lived near it. When we drove up in front of his dwelling he came out to where we were. He was a large, good-natured man and one that a stranger would have no trouble in forming an acquaintance. He spoke up immediately and said: "I am glad to see you in this western world. Last spring I put out a very large garden and I have a good one and if you will camp near here you can have all the vegetables you want without cost and if you want meat I have a smoke house full of bacon, and plenty of flour. These you can have at a very low price."

We thanked him and tarried a few days, while our

horses were resting as well as ourselves. One day, in conversation, he asked me my name and the state I emigrated from, and he said immediately.

"You, then, are a licensed minister in the Cumberland Presbyterian Church, for a gentleman by the name of Johnston, a minister also, told me you was on the road and would be along soon."

I afterwards became very well acquainted with him and found him to be an elder in the same church and a man who exerted an excellent influence wherever he was known. He was not a long, sour-faced Christian, but one who could enjoy a hearty laugh and tell as spicy an anecdote as any one. He was a true man among men and this is saying enough of any one.

CHAPTER XVIII.

A few years after this his name was placed on the temperance ticket as a candidate for the Legislature. He did not have much book learning, as he said, but was one of the best judges of human nature I ever saw. I heard him make one of his political speeches. There was a large concourse of people present and when he arose to speak he said:

"Mr. Chairman, the men opposed to me are men of learning, while I have but a small amount of that article, but I contend I have a decided advantage over them all; there are but very few men who understand real good language while everybody understands poor language."

When he said this they proposed three cheers for Sam Allen, which was given with a hearty good will. He certainly would have been elected had it not been that he was running on the temperance ticket. If men would vote as they pray and they know is right the temperance ticket would be elected without much trouble, but party carries the day whether right or wrong, and while this is the case good men must take a back seat. These things will be changed after awhile when party must give place to right-thinking and right-acting.

After camping at the Abiqua a few days we passed beyond the Santiam river in search of winter quarters and work. South of this stream we found a beautiful country and only occupied here and there with inhabitants. A Mr. Wm. Earl proposed to me that we could occupy the upper portion of his house for the winter and what work he had he would give it to me. It was not long until we had a home of our own and moved into it.

In the spring there was to be a political county convention held in Albany, the county town of Linn county, and my friend Earl was anxious that I should go and become a candidate for assessor. I told him I never had much to do with politics and that was not my object in coming west; that I would much rather remain in private life than to be tossed about on the uncertain sea of a political campaign. However, I went with him, was placed in nomination as a candidate and run for the office and was elected by a very large majority. So far as I ever knew the people, as a general thing, were satisfied, at least I suppose they were, for when they came to the next convention they wanted me to run for the same office but I stoutly refused. I felt then, and still feel, that one year of a political life was enough without going further and having character understood and men offering money if I would only use it at certain precincts. I think every man ought to do his duty at the polls and those offering bribes ought never to be allowed a vote. This constitutes all of my political life and I have always been glad it did, for there is a host who are ruined morally and who become drunkards just because they have been political aspirants and held some petty office I was then quite young and although raised right I might have gone astray with all my Scotch stubbornness had I entered heart and soul into politics. I never could swim in water and I think I should have made just as poor one on the political sea. I felt that I had another and greater calling than to enter political strife and that God's claims were far above all others and that wish should be followed.

I gave myself to the work of preaching and trying to save men from endless ruin I remember once establishing an appointment on North Santiam and one Sunday I preached on endless punishment, proving the doctrine from the Bible and showing its reasonableness. There was present a Universalist and after the sermon he said to a neighbor, "I do not believe in scaring people into religion."

"Oh," said the other, "if they can be scared into it let them be scared for it will be the happiest scare they ever had in all their lives."

Now, I want to talk a little while to any young minister who may chance to read this article. I had an appointment once for what was then termed a two days' meeting at the Elkins school house in what was known as the Forks of Santiam. My two days' meeting was begun on Saturday night. Through the week I had been trying to fix up a sermon for the first appointment and all the text I could find to interest me was the one found in the book of Daniel, "Thou art weighed in the balances and art found wanting " All I could think about was the history connected with the text and when I got up to preach I had no trouble going that far. When I had gone that far the thought occured to me. "now what are you going to do with the balances and what will you place on each side " Put an ungodly world on one side and God's law on the other and see how they will balance. I never had better liberty in preaching in all my experience and I wound up by showing that Christ alone could balance the scales as he was the end of the law for righteousness to every one that believeth.

When the sermon was finished they came running to me telling what a fine sermon they had. The thought occured to me, "you call that a good sermon I will show what a good one is tomorrow." The morrow came and a full house assembled and I took for a text, "And I saw, as it were, a sea of glass mingled with fire; and them that had gotten the victory over the beast, and over his image, and over his mark, and over the number of his name stands thereon having the harps of God." If there was a sea of glass I never saw it and I never got anywhere near the harps of God; but I quit badly whipped and, to a certain extent, pride conquered, although I have had many a hard tussle with it since. But it learned me one very important lesson and that was to take plainer texts and not try to show my own smartness instead of preaching Christ.

There was a camp meeting once held by the United Brethen a few miles from where I lived and I attended it on the sabbath. They asked me to preach for them in the afternoon, which is and always has been, a very unfavorable hour. However, I consented and took for a text, "For the bed is shorter than that a man can stretch himself on it and the covering narrower than that he can wrap himself in it." When I got up to preach the people were standing in groups talking, or seated eating melons, not all the congregation but perhaps one-half. I told them I was not sure whether I had anything to say that would interest them but one thing was sure my experienc of text would not fail to interest all if they would listen and hear it. They commenced to be seated and finally all were ready to listen and when I told what the text was some came near laughing out loud. There was a good degree of interest and excellent attention but the thing I wanted to speak of particularly was this: There was present a gentleman and his wife whom I did not know and had never met and after the sermon they started for home a few miles distant. After they left the camp ground and were traveling homeward they both seemed to be very serious. Finally the husband broke the silence and said:

"Wife, somebody has been telling that preacher all about us having that orphan boy and how bably we are treating him by furnishing the bed we have. We must mend our ways and get him a better bed and better covering so that we will not be exposed next time we attend church."

It was not long before the poor fellow had as good a bed as other boys.

The winter of 1856 and 1857 was one of the worst I ever saw in any country for dampness. There were forty days without one single ray of bright sunshine and it rained some out of every twenty-four hours. We resolved to go where there was sunshine if it was to be found on the western slope of our great country. When we left Oregon for California, which was in February, 1858, the elder of the church where I had been preaching for several years and in whose bounds we lived came to me and said:

"You are going into a very dangerous country, one where human life is not valued very highly and it will be necessary for you to be well armed or they are sure to kill you."

I told him I was not the least afraid of any thing of the kind, that it did not look well for a minister of the gospel of peace to tell men to repent, and at the same time have a Bible in his pocket and a pistol in the other ready to defend himself and kill others.

Said he with still more earnestness: "I do not want you to leave Oregon without a pistol and I have one that I will make you a present of. It needs to be repaired a little, which you no doubt can have done at Portland while you are waiting for the steamer."

He placed the pistol in my satchel and said: "You must get this repaired for no doubt you will want it in your new home."

I did not see the weapon again until after we had been in California some time.   We had some fowls which the owls were troubling at night.   I had the pistol repaired and used to shoot at the owls so as to frighten them away.   It would hardly have killed even if it had hit the owls for it was nothing but an old Allen "pepper box." One night when we were all gone from home some one broke into the house and stole a pair of blankets, a chopping ax, a watch, a fine tooth comb, fifty cents in money and the pistol and that was the last I saw of them.

I have related the above for the purpose of showing the opinion that even good men had in those days about California society.   Then this state was looked upon as being inhabitated by a cut-throat race of people and one especially dangerous to travel in, or to live in.   I never found any trouble in traveling through any of this western country and I have traveled thousands of miles on horseback and in a buggy, by steamers and railroads.   I have found Californians a whole-souled people and willing to entertain strangers, and as to morals they will compare favorably with any of the newer states and territories, or even with Oregon, our neighbor on the north, although the Portland Oregonian may entertain different views.   I once talked with a lady who came down from Oregon to California on a visit to some friends.   I said to her:

"When I lived in Oregon I liked the society very much.   Most of the people attended church, and rich and poor met on an equality.   A stranger could not tell the rich from the poor at their social gatherings."

'If you were there now, sir, you would find a line drawn and that the rich were greatly stuck up," she replied.

My candid opinion is that great improvements could be made both in Oregon and California society and the one has no right to boast over the other. Every lover of good morals loves to hear of men everywhere quitting evil practices and learning a language that has an elevating tendency, and not one tending downward, for the interest of one is in the same sense the interest of all and the downfall of one may cause the downfall of many more. No one, it matters not how rich and learned he is, is authorized to hold his head so high that he forgets he is traveling on the earth and liable to tramp on his neighbors corns. Until the discovery of gold in California money was a very scarce article in Oregon. But when gold was discovered in California, Oregon began to wake up and the blood went rushing through her veins with increased speed and her strong arm was pushed out in many enterprises for the benefit of this western country. If Oregon can surpass us in the way of morals and enterprise all right. But be sure, our neighbors of the north who dwell in a colder climate, that you are willing to give us equal chances with yourselves and then if we can beat you in the way of morals and sobriety and in pushing out in all directions with our great enterprises we are going to do it and if in after years you find yourselves in the shade and see us in the bright sunshine enjoying the golden hues, just conclude that it was our push and courage that made us what we are as well as our "glorious climate."

The journey from Oregon to California was a very stormy one, in fact the captain, although he was an old sailor on this coast, said the ocean was rougher than he ever saw it. We were ten days from the mouth of the Columbia river to San Francisco, a trip that is now made in less than three days.

We arrived in California in February, 1858, and as soon as we passed through the Golden Gate the sun commenced shining and revealing the country around the bay. After ten days of rough, stormy weather and strong head winds it was cheerful to find such a great change. We made our way, the same day of our arrival in San Francisco, to Stockton and I commened to look around and see what could be done in religious matters. I found a small church organized about seven miles from Stockton on the Sacramento road and finding a vacant house we moved among them and commenced work. There was no church organized in Stockton by the C. Ts., and, of course, no building in which to hold services. After consulting with a few members who lived there we concluded to make an effort to build.

Stockton then had a population of about 1000 and there were two Methodist church buildings and one Presbyterian. Our first effort was to find a lot on which to erect a house of worship. This was soon done and we started our subscription paper and in a few months the building was erected, house and lot paid for and a church organized The elder, a Mr. Horsman, assisted me in all the work, except he would not go into saloons and beg money for church purposes. I went into every saloon in the town and my recollection now is that I never failed to get money out of any of them. Sometimes I would find them gambling and watch them a few moments and say:

"Gentlemen, I am a stranger in this country but I have always understood that men following your occupation were very liberal toward the churches, and as I am trying to build one in this city I called to get some help, 'now show us your hand, if you please,'" and they generally responded very liberally.

While I was engaged in the building enterprise in town I kept up a regular appointment at my home place and also established an appointment at Woodbridge, a small town eight miles north. Sabbath then in California was the great day for drinking, card playing and horse racing and Woodbridge was no exception to the rule. This town was named in honor of a man who used to keep a hotel there by the name of Wood. There was no preaching there and my recollection is that I held the first religious services ever held in the place. There was a school house not far from town where ministers sometimes preached. At my first appointment a member and one of the elders went with me, as they said for a kind of "body guard." There had been a Masonic hall erected and they kindly consented that services might be held in the lower portion of it. When we arrived we found we were the only persons who had come to church. I confess it looked very discouraging about keeping up a regular appointment. We waited for some time but there were no additions to the congregation. As miners say, I very soon resolved to go out

on a prospecting tour and not give the matter up.   Not
far from the hall I found a saloon full of men drinking
and gambling.   I went back and told those who came
with me that I thought I would go over and invite them
to church.

"Yes, you do that," they both replied, "and you will
get whipped before you get out of the saloon You must
remember you are a very late arrival in California and
are not accustomed to the ways of the people here."

I replied that I was not the least afraid of being
whipped, that that was a game two could play at and I
had determined to risk the consequences and go. I went
over and walked into the saloon and watched them gam-
ble and drink a few moments and then pulled off my hat
and made them as polite a bow as I could (after I had
called their attention.) Then I said to them, "gentlemen, you have had a game of your kind, now come over
to church at the hall and take a game of my kind."   I
also gave the bartender a special invitation to come, and
he said immediately:

"I request every one present to get out of here and go
to church for I want to close the saloon as soon as possible and go out and get my family and attend church, for
no man shall come into my saloon and invite me but
what I must hear what he has to say."

I returned and told my companions what I had done
and that they were nearly all coming to church, but still
they doubted and I told them to wait a few moments and
see.   It was only a short time until they commenced to
come, and with them the saloon keeper and his family.
Others saw them coming and they also came until the

congregation numbered about eighty, and as well-be-
haved as any one could wish. There was one man, who,
I think, had one dram beyond sober, came in eating a red
apple. He seated himself but kept on eating and looking to see what I was going to do. He finally laid his
apple and knife down by his side and listened, seemingly
with an intense interest, until the close of the services
and then resumed his eating. The text I preached from
that day was a very pointed one, ''And those shall go
away into everlasting punishment.'' It never entered
my mind that such a text, owing to the occasion, might
be regarded as a direct insult, until afterwards when I
got to thinking about it.

From the text I endeavored to show the real necessity
there was for inflicting punishment in the world to come,
that no government on earth was safe without it and
that God in his infinite goodness would inflict punishment in the future on all who refused submission to His
will while they lived.

Second—I endeavored to show the nature of the punishment to the inflicted   That one of the main ingredi-
ents would be the lashings of a guilty conscience and
the fact that there was nothing in all the universe to
calm its fears, that such has passed out and beyond
God's compassion and that consistently with his nature
mercy could not be extended to them. I asked those
who drank how they would like to have the raging thirst
for liquor to continue to haunt them forever and yet no
means of gratifying it. Or then how would you like to
have the influence and power that gambling has over you
to continue for interminable ages, tossing the soul about

as if on a sea of fire. I contended that wrong-doing
made men miserable here and where it would be continued in the world to come and all by their own acts
they must of necessity continue to be miserable, for look
where they would they would not see relief coming to
them. I urged that if hell was no worse than a troubled
conscience, which in its very nature was tormenting, that
it was better to shun it.

Third—I endeavored to show the duration of the punishment, taking for my authority the text, ''And these
shall go away into everlasting punishment.'' When I
advanced to this proposition there was a silence and
solemnity which was almost oppressive.

After that day I never had any trouble in securing a
congregration at that place as long as I preached there
and was always treated with respect by the people, including the saloon keeper. They seemed to respect me
the more because I told them the truth as found in God's
word. This, I suppose, was the beginning of what is
now known as the Woodbridge church where our good
brother, Dr. Steen, now ministers and has been minis-
tering in holy things for a number of years past. After
the scenes of that day they sent me an invitation to come
and deliver a temperance address. I took some good
singers with me and went and their were, I think, fourteen who enlisted with the Sons of Temperance. It was
quite a temperance revival for a small, new town and I
hope done some good. There is no doubt but what the
singing of temperance songs added greatly to the interest
of the evening's entertainment.

CHAPTER XIX.

I believe it is a historical fact that the first camp meeting ever held in Christendom was held in July, 1800, by a Presbyterian minister whose name was McGready and that the custom was kept up by them for a number of years. Finally it was taken up by the Cumberland Presbyterians and Methodists and has by them been carried on until the present day. Camp meetings in an early day, when houses of worship were scarce, were no doubt productive of great good, but their utility does not appear so plainly in the older sections of our country where houses of worship are so abundant.

In September, 1858, assisted by others ministers I held a camp meeting near the Calaveras river about five miles from Stockton and not very far from the road leading from Stockton to Sacramento city and the bounds of the congregation where I was preaching. The first service seemed to be an indication of what the future ones would be. The Spirit of the Lord was present with His moving power uniting the hearts of God's people as the heart of one man. It was largely attended by the people of Stockton who seemed deeply interested in the services. Although some of the rougher element were present yet such was the deep solemnity which pervaded the entire audience they behaved as well as though they had been inside of a house of worship. The preaching was of a very plain, practical kind, mostly on doctrine showing the foundation on which the Church of God rested. Human responsibility was clearly pointed out showing that God alone had the righ

to our services. I believe there would be more conversions at the present time if the great doctrines of our
holy religion were explained more and defended by those
who stand on Zion's walls to proclaim God's eternal
truth. It was when the Apostles preached "Jesus and
the Resurrection" that men in great numbers turned to
the Lord. On the day of Pentecost the preaching was
doctrinal and that of the strongest kind, "Him being
delivered by the determinate counsel and foreknowledge
of God ye have taken and by wicked hands have crucified
and slain whom God hath raised up, having loosed the
pains of death because it was not possible that he should
be holden of it." It was when Paul "reasoned of righteousness, temperance and judgment to come that Felix
trembled." And it does seem to me there is no other
way to make men tremble only in view of their responsibility and the coming scenes of the final judgment as
revealed in the Holy Bible.

During the meeting to which I refer there were no
great, noisy demonstrations such as is sometimes common on such occasion, but an awful solemnity seemed to
hover about the grove in which the meeting was held
and it prevaded every heart, whether they were professors or not. I remember one man who lived eighty miles
from town who said he had important interests to see to
in Stockton. For six days in succession he made an
effort to go to town and when he came near the meeting
he said there was an invisible power which restrained
him and he would remain at the meeting during the day.
This man was not a professor of religion but he felt the
moving of God's Spirit and a loud call to God's

Service. Whether he was yielded or not I do not know.

The result of that meeting, so far as visible things were concerned, was thirty conversions and accessions to the church and among the number was a young man who afterwards become a minister of the gospel and is still holding up the standard of the Cross. This young man was convicted of sin in rather a peculiar manner. Together with a number of other men he was engaged in teaming from Stockton to the mines. One night a number of these teamsters met at a certain hotel and after supper was over and their teams attended to they all assembled in the barroom. At times it was the custom for all who could sing, to sing a song before retiring for the night. As a rule these songs were not of a religious nature. One and another had sung their songs until the last one to sing was the young man to whom I refer. Before he sang remarks were made complimenting the singers and all seemed to have a great amount of sport as they joined in their merry peals of laughter at the songs and the singers, when all, with united voice, said to the young man, "Now, Lat, it is your turn to give us a song." He was an excellent singer and had been raised in a deeply pious family in his native state. He said he never knew why it was, but he selected the song that had thrilled so many hearts in the ages past, "Amazing Grace How Sweet the Sound that Saved a Wretch Like Me; I once was Lost but now I'm Found; was Blind but not I See." He sung all six verses and when he had finished he was left alone in the room, for, one by one, they had all retired. This was the arrow

the Holy Spirit used to reach his soul, although there
was not a word spoken by any one, but all retired to rest
in deep silence and amid deep solemnity. There was
but little rest for him for his song brought up memories
of other days, when the family were assembled for their
accustomed evening worship and among the songs they
used to sing was the one he had just repeated. This was
the means used to bring him to Christ.

During the meeting, one night about 12 o'clock, I was
awakened by the voice of prayer which came from a man
who seemed to be alive to the danger his soul was in of
being forever lost. It was only a few moments until a
messenger arrived saying, "The man who keeps the
boarding tent wishes to see you." This man was a
cripple in one of his arms and had resorted to the saloon
business for a living and was keeping one almost in
sight of the camp ground. We made him promise not
to sell any liquor during the meeting and gave him the
boarding tent. He kept his word and conducted an
orderly house at the meeting. The night of which I
have already spoken he seemed to have an awful view of
his sins and the evil he had done in selling whiskey.

When I came to him he seemed to be greatly alarmed
and cried out, "Parson, pray for me for I shall soon be
beyond help."

"Mr. W.," said I, "are you willing to quit selling that
which is ruining you as well as many others and become a meek and lowly follower of the Redeemer?"

"No, Parson," said he, "I cannot give that up; if I did
I would starve "

"Do you not believe God could find some other way

Going down Laurel Hill.—page 59.

for you to make a living?"

"No, I do not see how he could."

I told him very plainly he could not be a Christian and live only to sell that which had proved the ruin of so many thousands; that with such work he could not glorify God. His agony seemed to increase and I pleaded with the Lord to give him courage to come out boldly on the Lord's side.

It was all of no avail; he would not give up his evil ways and trust the Lord to show him a better way. After this he never swore himself, neither would he allow any one to swear who was in his employ. Not many years after this he was found dead in bed one morning, having died with delirium tremens, it was thought, for he had been showing symptons of them for some little time. When I first formed his acquaintance he told me he had a wife in the states and that she belonged to the "High Pressure Church." I told him that was a new church to me and he would have to explain himself. He said, "the 'High Pressure Church' was the Methodist church because they loved to shout so loudly."

The last time I ever saw him was a year or two after I had moved away. I was passing one day and as I halted to water my horse he came out and while we were talking an old neighbor rode up, and when he had watered his horse, he said:

"Parson, come in and have a horn with me, for you never drank with me while you lived here."

"No, I never did," said I, "and should I go in and drink with you now you would feel like 'hooting' me out of the place for you know it is wrong for a minister of the gospel to drink."

However, I went into the saloon and got a drink of water and the saloon keeper gave me a cigar. When the neighbor went to pay for his dram he handed me five dollars saying I was traveling and it might come very handy for expenses. As he did this the saloon keeper threw down a dollar and a half making the same kind of a remark.

Two or three weeks after the camp meeting near Stockton there was one held near the town of Mountain View in Santa Clara county. The ground was nicely shaded with trees which afforded a good shelter for those who came to worship. The meeting began on Friday and without any religious interest so far as man could judge. Saturday the attendance was greatly increased but the interest remained the same both at morning and evening services. Sabbath was a beautiful day and after the morning prayers at the tent and breakfast was over there was a general prayer meeting held before the hour of preaching. After the 11 o'clock sermon the sacrament of the Lord's Supper was administered but the services seemed to all to be lifeless. Even unconverted men began to talk about it saying: "I was in hopes there would be a deep interest on the part of the Christian people so that we might feel like becoming Christians for it cheers us as well as them to see life in the services."

The afternoon services proved to be like those going before and professors of religion and non-professors both seemed to grow restless about it, wondering what the

outcome would be.   Between the afternoon and evening
service two young ministers had gone for a walk and to
talk about the meeting when they were overtaken by
the leader of the meeting (sometimes they were called
Bishops even if they were Presbyterians)   This Bishop
was Father Brawley who said, "Brethern, I was searching for you, one of you must preach tonight and I cannot determine which shall. so you must settle it between
yourselves," and took his departure.   The two young
men retired to separate places and prayed and then they
came together again but neither was satisfied.   Again
they went and prayed and when they met again the
younger of the two said, "For the first time in my life
life I believe I am the one who should preach the sermon
tonight."

"If you have the light, preach, for I am not at all satisfied," said the other.

The hour arrived for the evening service to begin and
with a heart full of his message he entered the pulpit
and began   When he commenced he told the congregation:

"When I have finished what I have to say I expect to
ask those who desire to be saved to come forward for the
prayers of God's people, and a number are coming and
they are going to experience the joys of pardoned sins,
and I want you Christian people to be ready to pray
with them and then lead them to Christ and rejoice with
them."

The leader, or Bishop of the meeting, was an old vet-
eran and had passed through many spirtual conflicts but
the assertion of the young minister seemed almost to

unnerve him and he groaned aloud, so as to be heard
over the encampment, and said afterwards he thought
all was ruined and a declaration made that would not be
fulfilled. The brother, he thought, must be beside himself when he already knows there has not been any interest at the meeting.

The preaching was of the heart-searching kind and
told plainly as words could make it what would be the
condition of the finally impenitent in the future and that
their only hope was in Christ, who was waiting and
willing to save them then and now.

At the close of the sermon the call for seekers of religion was made as promised and six came forward and
all were converted before midnight. Among the number
who came forward was one who had been an avowed infidel, talking his infidelity to his neighbors. He lived
not far from the Bishop of the meeting. He said the
night services had convinced him of the reality of religion
and he wanted to find Christ. He made his way to the
leader of the meeting and while on his bended knees
and his eyes streaming with tears he looked up at him
and said:

"Father Brawley, pray for me for I am a poor, undone
sinner about to be lost. You know I have long slighted
these things and said I was an infidel; God pity me
and have compassion on me. Oh, pray for me."

The appeal was successful and Father Brawley knelt
and I certainly never heard him pray with such earnestness as he did that night. He seemed to bring heaven
and earth together. There was no longer dullness in
the meeting but life from the Spirit of God. It was only

a short time until the power of the Highest was made known in the conversion of the infidel. Men who had been his intimate companions gathered about him and looked on astonished at the lightning up of his countenance and it made them, too, feel that religion was a devine reality. The six who came forward for prayers all made a profession before midnight and from that time on until the close of the meeting there were many more saved. God wants all his ministers to be deeply in earnest when they deliver their message to their fellow men for eternal interests are involved. The leader of that meeting and his once infidel neighbor have both gone to their eternal home, we trust, amid the glories and beauties of the heavenly land.

In 1860 I was appointed as agent for the college previously located at Sonoma, one of the old towns of California. That fall we moved to Sonoma valley, a beautiful country to look at but rather a hard place for a poor man to make a living. In my judgment there were better locations for a denominational college than this one and one where it would have prospered and did great good. A wine producing community such as Sonoma was then, and still more so in after years, was by no means favorable for the morals of the youth who lived there and who might come there to be educated; but the Synod had selected it and I acquiesced in the decision although the selection was made before I came to California. The first sessions of the school were held in an old Adobe building whose exterior was anything but beautiful but whose interior had been furnished in a more becoming manner. I said the Synod had selected the location. It was the

Pacific Presbytery, and afterwards when the Synod was organized they approved the selection also.

The corner stone of the new building, I think, was laid the fall of 1860 under the direction of the Masonic fraternity, Dr. W. A. Scott delivering the address. The new building was to be 50x70 feet and three stories in height, including the roof. The foundation was to be of rock, and at first it was the intention to have erected a stone building but this was changed afterwards and a concrete one was put up in its stead. There is no building anywhere that could have a more secure place on which to build, for although the foundation was built of rock it rested on rock all around the building. It is a substantial building with a flat roof and one that presents a good appearance to the passer by. While I was acting as agent for it I told the trustees one day that I was going over to a Mr. Swift's, a very wealthy man living on the west side of the valley, to see what could be done in the way of getting means from him. I remained and took dinner with him by his own invitation. When we started for the dining room he went to the mantel piece and took from it his Bourbon bottle and wanted me to take a dram.

"No, sir, I never tasted it in my life and I will not begin now," I said.

"Oh, it will not do you any harm," he replied. I refused.

"Mr. S.," said I "you would be a great deal better off today had you never had anything to do with it."

"I believe men are much better off who do not use it, but I have become so accustomed to it that I have no appetite to eat unless I drink it," was his answer. He down with his dram and we went to dinner and had a real nice social time. After dinner he showed me his buildings, consisting of a stone barn, a stone fish pond and a stone house. He wanted me to see his library room where he was erecting a book case and expected that it and his library would cost $10,000, and yet he could neither read nor write. After showing me these things we took a seat on the front porch, for it was a warm, pleasant day and I said to him:

"With all your beautiful surroundings I would fully expect to get $2000 for our college here in the valley and near your home."

"I do not think I can give you as much as that," said he "but I will give you $1000, for I would like to see a good college here for the benefit of the valley."

The school was moved from the old Adobe building to the new one as soon as it was ready to be occupied. It seemed to be prosperous for a time, but after awhile the trustees borrowed some money and mortgaged the building and lot to a private individual and it was not long until the entire property was lost to the church, and finally the party purchasing sold it to the school district and it is now used as a high school. I continued as agent for two years and then resigned and it was several years after this when the property changed hands and was lost so far as the church was concerned. Now the church has no organization in the valley, neither does it own any property there.

While living in Sonoma valley I used to preach at St. Helena in Napa county, occasionally. The winter of

1861 I went there to hold meetings Saturday and Sunday but the interest was such that they continued for three weeks. It was very rainy weather, but those living at a distance put covers on their wagons and came although there was no moonlight. Every night the house was well-filled and it was plainly to be seen that the interest was gradually increasing.

There was a young lawyer living in the community who had been raised in a very pious family, his father being a Presbyterian minister in the city of Philadelphia and pastor of a large church. He had left home when quite young and had sailed in almost all waters finally finding a stopping place in one of the mountain counties of California where he married an excellent Christian women. He got into the habit of drinking some before he entered on a political career and of course the excitement of political life only urged it on. He was elected to the California Legislature and while in Sacramento he drank to such excess that he had the delirium tremens, or, as Father Denny of Oregon used to term it, "devil's trimmings." The doctor was called and he forbid him having any more liquor. He told me he was worth at the time about $5000 and that he offered all this for one bottle of brandy, which was refused him After his term expired in the Legislature he moved to St. Helena where I made his acquaintance. He had become sober but had turned infidel and was arguing it with his neighbors. The meeting had been going on some ten days and although his wife attended he did not go himself. I was stopping with one of the elders of the church and one day it was raining as usual and I got up, put on my overcoat and gathered an umbrella, when he called out, "where are you going in such a rain as this." I told him I was going to see the judge.

"You had better stay in out of the rain for it is a very foolish errand on which you are going for that man is an infidel and you will only make a failure."

"No," said I, "I feel that I must go."

I went and found him in his office all alone and after a little pleasant conversation I said to him: "Judge, I believe I have a message from God for you tonight and I would be pleased to see you." He replied immediately.

"I will be there, sir."

He came according to promise and the sermon was on the Law of God. It seemed to interest him and that night before the close of the meeting he was converted and went to preaching and has been a faithful minister of the gospel ever since and the instrument in God's hands of the conversion of thousands, for it has been almost a constant revival under his ministery since that time. At that same meeting there was a child converted only eight years old and rather timid. She was helped on to a seat where for some time she talked about religion and the love of God in the soul until all who heard her were astonished at her wisdom in view of her tender years. Also there was a young lady who was engaged to be married who became insensible and many thought she was going to die. Her lover went for the doctor and when he came he said it would take a higher power than him to do anything with a case of that kind. She lay there, perhaps, two hours, and such was the interest in her condition that the services ceased, only a song was sung occasionally. Finally she showed signs of life and it was only a moment until she could tell how happy a soul was with Jesus formed in the hope of glory. The doctor was a good, religious man and a member of the Baptist church and when she commence talking, he said, "I knew it would all be right."

CHAPTER XX.

Now it is 1862 and April 10th has arrived, the day set for the departure of a company of men for the northern mines and as the country is greatly agitated about the civil war it seems to be a favorable time to try the fortune in the gold fields. When one has worked for the public until debts accumulate then he had better work for himself awhile and try to gain a little of the world's goods and pay up, rather than be regarded as either carless or negligent about paying his just liabilities.

We left the beautiful valley of Sonoma and determined to cross the country to the Powder river mines in eastern Oregon, in preference to going by water to the Dalles and then overland. And now it will be necessary to take the reader over another range of mountains differing considerably from either the Rocky Mountains or the Cascades, although there is a similarity in all mountain ranges. We traveled up the Sacramento river by way of Red Bluff and found excellent grass all the way. In almost all companies of men there is sure to be at least one who is a fine talker and takes great delight in exhibiting his loquacious talent to his traveling com-

panions. We had one of this kind in our company
whose tongue (if such a thing was possible) seemed to
be hung on a hinge or pivot in the middle and when one
end tired try the other. He was well informed, or at
least could talk about any subject which might be
named, and he delighted in telling what he knew and he
could do it to very good advantage. He had but little
force of character and very often intruded himself on un-
willing listeners. Talk he would and take he did and it
seemed like you might as well try to dam up the Sacramento river in time of a flood as to check the onward
current which came from him, for it seemed to pour
from him as naturally as water in a swift current, for
difficulties did not stop him and if he happened to rest
awhile it was only to gather strength for an onward
flight of oratory When awake he talked almost incess-
antly, and certainly a man who could keep up such a
rapid incessant roar must have spent most of the night
in thinking what to say the next day. He was one of
the kind who did not repeat what he had said before but
seemed to have a fresh supply for each day as we journeyed on. One day we tarried for noon in a most beautiful meadow and after lunch had been disposed of and
while our horses were eating, this talkative man came
where I was. I was sitting on the grass in a very com-
fortable frame of mind when he came and threw himself
down at full length, with his head resting in my lap,
and looking up at me as innocent as a child and asked,
"Parson what do you think of me anyhow."

"I think you are a regular gaspipe," I replied.

This only seemed to be the means of loosening his

tongue and of spuring him into greater activity than ever.

"Gaspipe," said he, "I am glad you said it, for there is no human invention that is much more useful than a gaspipe. When the city is wrapt in the sable shades of night and neither moon or stars to give light to the inhabitants then the gas comes along silently in the pipe until it reaches the proper place when it burns and throws out a beautiful light, saving the pedestrians from harm. Then look how that cottage is lit up affording the inmates great pleasure in reading. But come again to your beautiful mansion and see its magnificent parlor lighted up too with gas. Father, mother, a son and a daughter are there enjoying the evening as only families can, when a young man, neatly clad and in whose looks tales of love can be read, enters and takes a seat with the group. The parents and the son soon retire and leave the two young people to themselves. There in the light afforded by that gaspipe he whispers words of love into her ears and could you peep in you would see two intense lovers enjoying that which flows from that light He gets a little nearer to her for he wants to ask her a very important question and not too loudly for fear some one might be listening. His heart flutters and he almost pants for breath but after awhile his nerves become a little steadier and his courage assumes a firmer hold and he asks, 'do you love me enough to become a life partner? Will you be mine?' Now his heart beats faster than ever while she hesitates for a moment and the crimson tide rushes to her cheeks, but she finally says, 'yes, I will be yours.' Oh such wonderful happiness, such joy, such delightful ecstasy, and all the result of the gas-pipe."

"Again," said he, "let us go to the house of the Lord where an elequent divine is preaching God's eternal truth, let us enter, how beautiful the light is here and it all comes from the gaspipe. See that immense congregation of worshipers as they sing the songs of Zion until divine melody fills the room. See the man of God as he rises with a solemn countenance and reads the word of the Lord and then says, 'Let us pray.' His prayer is soul-inspiring and when it concludes the congregation feels nearer heaven and that they are where Jesus is. Look at him as he stands there the very messenger of heaven, sent to tell men how to be roconciled to God. See how intently they listen so as not to miss any of the words he utters. He speaks of life and its responsibilities, the dangers of delay, that now is the accepted time and the day of salvation. Look again, some have accepted the invitation and now see the angels on joyful wings making their way to the celestial hills to tell that the 'dead is alive and the lost is found.'"

By this time the entire company has come near enough to listen, when I called out: "Hold! hold I am badly beaten and certainly I will never call any one else a gas-pipe, unless I think he is very useful to his fellow men."

The company all roared with laughter at my expense and said, "well, the Parson acknowledges he is beat for once." This incident afforded more or less sport for the company for hours to come. Such scenes as I have here

described helps very much to break the monotony of a
tedious journey and to drive away the blues.

CHAPTER XXI.

In our travels we passed the town of Redding which
was then a small village consisting of a blacksmith shop,
a hotel and a saloon, with but few dwellings. When we
came to the mouth of Pitt river where it empties into the
Sacramento we went up the former stream. In going
on the old emigrant road up this stream we sometimes
found pitts dug, the work of Indians in former days.
They would dig them and then cover them over so they
could not be told from the ground surrounding them.
Their original plan was to drive a stake in these pits and
sharpen the upper end so that if and elk or deer or bear
came along the trail it would fall on this pointed stick,
or then if any of the horses of the Hudson bay company
came along and fell on one of these sticks it would rejoice the hearts of the Indians, for then they
knew they would have meat for days to come. The
Hudson bay company used to be in that country trap-
ping.

One day as we passed along, not suspecting any
harm, an Irishman found one of these pits to his sorrow
for his horse fell into it and his legs were wedged fast
between the sides of the pit and the animal, until he
could not help himself. It was really comical to look at
his disturbed face. For once Pat was badly frightened
for he did not know what was in the pit. As soon as he
had sufficiently recovered from his fright to talk he

called out, "Gintlemen, will ye ones stand by and see a maun die and niver attempt to help a divil of a bit." It was only a few moments until men with shovels went to work and relieved him of his distress and he went on his way declaring "That any human beings who would dig such places ought to have vengeance meeted out to them, and then to cover them over so as to catch a poor Irishman going to the mines to make his fortune so as to support his wife and babies in a dacent manner. Wy, gintlemen, it is a great wonder that I had not been kilt outright and buried in one of them. It is too bad ontirely, so it is."

One night when we were camped on Pitt river the snow fell about six inches in depth, and those who had no tent to sleep in but only a blanket stretched over their heads, found in the morning that they had slept unusually warm. That morning we waited until the snow melted away and it was about noon before we resumed our journey. Some of the men, including the captain of our company who was an old Rocky Mountain trapper and used to Indians, concluded they would go out on a hunt. The captain had a desire to see whether the men would fight if they were to get into a dangerous place. He stationed himself behind a tree and acted the Indian, both in word and gesture. Finally some of the men saw him and drew their guns and fired, hitting the tree, but the captain had gone on the opposite side and was safe. After they had all got back to camp he told it and then added, "you will do to depend on if we should get into a battle."

As we went onward a few miles there was a large body

of smoke which would puff up and then die down, puff and then disappear again, and our captain exclaimed: "Men, that smoke comes from the signal fires of the Indians and every man of you look well to your guns and see that they are in the best possible condition for shooting, for we are liable to have a fight most any time."

We all halted and fixed our weapons for war. We were traveling up a rather narrow valley on the river with towering mountains on either hand and every man was on the sharp lookout for fear of an attack. Some of the men were actually pale with fear and as I had no looking glass cannot tell how pale I was. No doubt all hearts beat faster, but with all of our timidity we kept marching forward with gun in hand ready to shoot any Indian who might be in that part of the country. We kept very still for fear we might wake some slumbering savages when, to our astonishment, we came to a very large boiling hot spring and found that it had been the cause of our alarm. It was about twenty-five feet in diameter and without any bottom so far as we could see. There was quite a large creek running from it and there was no vegetation growing for several rods on either side. There must have been a very hot region below that spring for their was sufficient heat in the waters to cook with.

After passing to the head of Pitt river, which in reality we found to be a large, beautiful sheet of water called Goose lake, we passed on and beyond the Sierra Nevada mountains keeping up the lake and not turning to the right over a high mountain as the emigrant road did.

We found some beautiful country bordering on this la' e
and after we passed the head of it we found a stream
which was called Eagle creek. It was greatly swollen
from the melting snows but we selected a narrow place
and felled some trees and built a temporary bridge and
passed over in safety, with the exception of one small
mule, and it fell into the water, lost its pack, swam down
stream nearly a mile and then landed, coming out on the
side we wanted it too and came back in a great hurry to
the company, braying at every jump. When it returned
it was interesting to watch its expressions of joy as it ran
from one animal to another until it found the particular
ones with which it had been traveling, when it suddenly
became satisfied.

Beyond this creek we camped in a juniper grove, some
of the timber being dead We wanted some dry wood
for camp fires and one man took his axe and commenced
chopping down a tree, when to his great amazement a
bunch of something, which had been wound up in a
blanket, came tumbling down at his feet. For a few
moments he was as nervous as Pat was down on Pitt
river and immediately ceased chopping and ran away
from it. Finally he was told by our captain, as well as
some others, that it was the custom of some of the Indian tribes to roll their dead in as small a compass as
possible and put them in the tree tops and tie them fast
there with ropes made of grass. The rope had rotted
and the jarring of the tree had thrown it down. We did
not unwrap the skeleton, neither did we place it back in
the tree. The man soon found there was no danger of
the dead Indian shooting him and proceeded to cut the

tree down.

We found good water and good timber both very scarce in that portion of Oregon. After we had crossed some streams and came to some mountains we found wood in abundance and good water and some appearance of gold, but not enough to justify us in stopping very long, for the Indians were troublesome in that part of the country. On our way to Powder river we passed through the John Day country where we saw indications of gold and which afterwards developed into a very good mining camp. It was there that I panned my first pan of dirt in search of gold in the presence of two old California miners who made all manner of sport of my awkwardness. But when I got through with it and they saw I had about five cents worth of the yellow metal they went to work with a will, even if they had been shaking with laughter a few moments before at my expense. From the Indian signs in that part of the country we concluded that we had better move on to Powder river, the land we had in view when we started from home. When we arrived at Auburn, a small village in that country, the first thing that arrested our attention was a sign over a saloon, not but what signs over saloon doors were very common, but this one was not common but very uncommon and one I had never seen before. "Mount Diabolo" in very large letters which had evidently been placed there by some Oregon man who did not understand the meaning of those two very significant words, for had he searched the dictionary thoroughly he certainly could not have found a more appropriate name.

The first Sunday after our arrival I preached under a large pine tree. There was thought to be about 500 present and with all that number their was only one lady, the wife of a Baptist minister. This seemed very odd and yet it was no uncommon occurence in the early days of mining in California. There is one thing that I think all ministers have noticed who have preached in the mines, and that is as a rule men are orderly and well behaved, even if but few ladies do attend, showing that the men can have good order without them.

During the summer and fall of 1862 a large emigration made their way across the plains from the western states and many found their way into the Powder river mines, so that during the following winter Auburn had quite a large population for a mining camp. All the houses were built of logs, as there was no saw mill near there at the time. Among the emigrants who came were four young men messmates from Colorado and one of their number was a Frenchman, a blacksmith by trade. He hired the other three, who were the owners of the wagon and team, to bring him and his tools to Powder river for the sum of $100. When they were at their journey's end he refused to pay them, according to contract, and they wanted to leave it to three disinterested men and let them decide what was right. Before they did this all four went out prospecting one day and in the afternoon the Frenchman, who returned first, took some flour from a sack, cooked it and ate his dinner and went away among some friends. After finishing his meal he put the contents of a vial of strychnine into the sack and carelessly dropped the vial near by. It so happened

that a lady who was camped near them saw all the movements of the Frenchman but at the time thought but
little, if anything, about the matter as she was busy with
her own work When the three returned they all came
together and the lady of whom I speak was absent from
her camp and did not see them return. Being very
hungry they commenced frying pancakes or as the miners call them, fla jacks, and to eat quite greedily for it
was well along in the afternoon and they had not eaten
anything since early breakfast. All of them partook of
the first cake fried, when one of them said, "Boys, there
is something wrong with this flour." When the second
cake was cooked a portion of it was given to their dog
and he very soon went into spasms. It was but a little
while until all three men were very sick and two of them
died in a short time. The doctors worked with the third
man the best they could and finally saved him from
death. Such news as this soon spread through the entire mining region and brought together a number of
people and among those who came was Judge Carver,
who was engaged with Messrs. Barlow and Rector in
viewing out the Barlow road across the Cascade Mountains into western Oregon, who was at the scene among
the first. It was very plainly to be seen that they had
been poisoned by some means. The lady mentioned
above said she saw the Frenchman put something into a
sack of flour from a vial and then drop it on the ground
near by and she believed if they would search for the
vial they would soon find it. The search was made, the
vial found branded strychnine with a grain of the deadly
drug still in it. The Frenchman was pointed out and

immediately taken into custody by a man appointed then and there for that purpose.

That night there was a mass meeting by the miners called to see what was best to be done. Judge Carver was elected chairman and by his counsel a sheriff was chosen, who proved to be the man who first took charge of the Frenchman. It was decided to appoint three judges and twelve jurymen to try him, as there was no county organization there and it was several hundred miles to the nearest county town. Judge Carver was appointed presiding officer. A regular licensed lawyer took charge of the case for the people and also one for the prisoner. The most important witness was the man poisoned, but not dead, and the court adjourned from day to day until he was able to attend. Finally the trial began, which caused a large audience to assemble at the appointed time.

After three days of fair and impartial trial, and as civil as though it had been a regularly organized court, the case was given to the jury who soon brought in a verdict of murder in the first degree. The presiding judge pronounced sentence in a very appropriate and solemn manner and then set the day and the hour for his execution.

Among the miners I never heard a doubt expressed about the condemned man's guilt, but all said he ought to hang. The Frenchman was a Catholic but as there was no priest in that part of the country I had to officiate for him as best I could. The night before his execution I went into the jail and talked to him until midnight and ate supper with him. I talked to him about his preparation for the future and that if he was guilty he ought to confess it and not keep denying it as he had done, that no one who did not tell the truth could ever enter that goodly land. 1 had to talk to him altogether through the aid of an enterpreter and whether he enterpreted right or not I had no means of knowing for I was not acquainted with the French language. According to the interpreter I did not succeed in convincing him that he had ever done any thing wrong in his life, although it was said that he had shot one man in Colorado.

The morning the execution took place was a beautiful one and the criminal refused to ride on his coffin but preferred to walk behind it. He was executed on a high hill near town so that all who wanted too could witness the scene. There was a large number of people present. The hardest task I ever had in religious matters was to go on to the scaffold and offer prayer for the condemned man. After he was placed on the trap he was asked if he had anything to say and to his interpreter he said, so he reported.

"Tell all the people I am going to die an innocent man. Write to my father and mother in France that I am innocent."

I offered prayer for him and at its close he handed me a gold watch, but I did not keep it long as it reminded me every time I took it from my pocket of the poor fellow hanging between heaven and earth. At the appointed time the cap was drawn, the rope adjusted and he fell and the only sign of life visible after his fall was the moving of one finger very slightly.

CHAPTER XXII.

The two years I was in the Powder river mines I held regular religious services morning and evening as a general rule. Mining through the week, when the weather would permit, and then preaching twice on the sabbath was hard work but I enjoyed it and the people seemed to appreciate it. Besides this work I took turns with others in publishing a monthly paper in manuscript form during the winter. The way the people obtained the news was to appoint a night for its reading, when large congregations would assemble and the editors would read the contents. This was a good many years ago but I believe the paper was named the Auburn News, in honor of the town in which it was published. I have often wished since that time that I had preserved a copy of it as a kind of literary curiosity of that day. It was frequently the case during the winter that men traveled forty miles on their snow shoes to listen to the reading, which occupied from one-half to two hours and yet they did not seem to tire or even grow restless. The paper contained articles on almost every subject, political, religious, mining matters and witticisms. The fun department was scattered all through the paper and seemed to keep up the interest when it was read. There were some excellent articles on the Whitman massacre, and probably the next article would be a Dutchman's courting adventure in western Oregon which would make all hands roar with laughter. Then there might be a good article on the old subject of temperance, followed by a description of the antics of a drunkard as he wiggled and staggered on his way home. The night the paper was to be read was known generally over the mining region and the only trouble was to secure a hall large enough to hold the people. Wedding notices, of course, came in for a full share and the notices were very elaborate. Once 1 went about twelve miles to marry a couple and although there were sixty present none knew of the wedding save the bride and groom and the bride's parents and a brother of the groom, but all had come dressed in common clothing to engage, as they supposed, in an old-fashioned candy pulling. All the ladies were dressed in plain calico, not expecting what was to take place. The bride and groom and the parents met in another house not far from the one where the guests were assembled and we all marched there with the couple to be married in front and as soon as they stepped into the room a few feet they turned round facing me and 1 went to saying the ceremony and they were soon united in marriage. Those assembled were greatly astonished, except the few who knew of the secret. One young lady declared afterwards that she did not catch her breath for at least five minutes. This incident was all written up in good style for the paper by an old writer and editor and when it was read there was one volley of applause after another.

It was too cold and the snow too deep for placer mining, which was the only mining done at that time, and such scenes as I have been describing greatly assisted in helping to pass away the long, tedious winter evenings. Through the day there was fun, any amount of it, running on snow shoes and this sport the Parson enjoyed as well as the rest. Some men made saloons their chief resort and played cards and drank whiskey, for the two seemed to be twin brothers, and thereby many young men were led astray and made to travel a downward path.

One day I wanted to get a book from the circulating library and had to go into a saloon to obtain it. Just as I stepped in the sheriff and judge with some others went to the bar for a drink and the saloon keeper said, "come, parson, have a drink with us and show yourself social for you have never tasted liquor since you came among us."

"You know, Mr. W.," I replied "If I should walk up to that bar and take a drink with you men that the respect you have for me as a minister of Christ would all vanish in a moment and you would be ready to say you never wanted me to preach to you again for you are not fit for such work."

"Parson," said the saloon keeper, "hold on until I give these men their drams and then I will talk to you."

After they had drank and passed out he came and seated himself by my side and said, "at home I did not follow this business but had a store where no liquor was sold and I was a class leader in the Methodist church and I thought I enjoyed those meetings as much as any one, but I was raised in the belief that I could get religion, as some term it, and then lose it again. When I came here I found no opening for making money but this and I did not like it and am determined to quit as soon as my stock of liquors is exhausted."

The cause of our alarm.—page 101.

I said to him, "you had better quit now for fear you might not live that long."

"Oh, 1 am not going to die in my present calling but you will see me reform before long."

"You have a hall above your saloon," said I, "will you let me have it for church purposes?"

"Yes," was the prompt reply, "you may have it free of rent and I will furnish the fuel, make the fires and keep it well lighted and swept."

He kept his word faithfully as long as we had the use of the hall but it soon proved too small to accommodate those who wished to attend and we rented another one but had to pay $25 a month for it. At the end of the month a collection was taken up and this saloon keeper was always one of the collectors. He would start the ball rolling by giving $5 himself and when the money was counted he always had more in his hat than any of the other collectors.

There are many men who once had noble, generous natures engaged in selling grog, but the difficulty is they are led on by degrees until their fallen natures gain the mastery over them and they are caught in the coils of the deadly serpent (rum) and are ruined.

The spring of 1863 I made a short trip into Idaho to see its mines and consult with a partner who had gone there before me. When I arrived at the main mining camp almost the first man I met was the same Mr. W., the saloon keeper spoken of above and that had been so kind to me at Auburn. I found him still selling whiskey and said to him, "I thought you was going to quit the business."

Said he, "Parson, my stock is not yet exhausted, I intend to be as good as my word."

I told him I had always found him so but supposed he had forgotten his promise, it had been so long sin e he made it.

"By no means; you will still find me true."

I do not know whether he had found out the secret of making one barrel of liquor do for several years or not, but it looked like it.

"Mr W., will you let me have your saloon to preach in tomorrow? You can cease selling drams for an hour, can you not?" I asked.

"Yes," said he, "I could, but I think I can find a better place for you to preach in than my saloon, but if I do not succeed you shall have it."

He went across the street to a building which was being erected for a barber shop; the front and one side both facing on the streets, had not yet been enclosed, and he said to the darkey, "How would you like to have preaching in your new shop tomorrow."

"Me like um fine, sah, me like to have um christened."

Before the hour for preaching arrived I asked a former Oregon neighbor, who was engaged in the auction business, if he would not go through town on a prancing steed and speak of it He kindly consented and at the appropiate time he went crying at the top of his voice "Preaching today at the new barber shop at 11 o'clock."

When the hour came I think there was the largest congregation assembled for worship that I ever saw anywhere. There was said to be 10,000 people in town that day and they crowded up as closely as they could

stand, for there were no seats, and as far as I could see
up and down the streets it was one vast sea of heads.
My voice then was excellent and I elevated it as high as
I knew I could control it. There was excellent order
and the best of attention to the gospel message and I
thought at the conclusion that the gospel had not yet
lost its power over the hearts of men. This was the second sermon ever preached in the town and I hope had
at least some good effects. The next morning a man
came to me and urged me to stay and do nothing but
preach; he said he had talked to a number of men and
they had concluded they could pay me at least $300 a
month. All these men, who were so desirous for me to
remain, showed by their countenance that they were
drinking men and some acted like they had too much
tanglefoot at the time they were talking with me and
beside all this I was at the time not situated so I could
remain.

A day or two after I left the town to return to Auburn two men went to shooting at each other. Before they had fired the first shot a Mr. Jones from southern Oregon ran up and tried to separate them, and as he
came up one of the combatants raised his pistol, with
the muzzle pointed back, getting ready to fire, when by
some means it was discharged, striking Mr. J. about the
center of the forhead killing him instantly. This was
the gentleman who acted as spokesman to me when they
asked me to remain with them. It was said that had he
been duly sober he would not have placed himself in
such a dangerous position. Whiskey sometime makes
men very bold and causes them to place themselves

where danger is found, and death overtakes them.

My friend Mr. W., who had gone from Auburn, continued in the saloon business for some time after my visit. One morning he failed to come to his breakfast when called and when they entered his room they found him dead. While selling liquor he got in the habit of drinking it and he kept on until delirum tremens finished his earthly career. It is very sad to see a generous hearted man and one who might be very useful engaging in a business that lashes his conscience and makes him wretched. This much I will say for this man, I never heard him utter an oath or say an unbecoming word of any one. He was uniformly kind to the poor and generous to a fault.

CHAPTER XXIII.

During the spring of 1863 there was a political meeting held at Auburn and a man who was afterwards elected to congress was the speaker. He was a man of fine appearance and quite large, but the most bitter man I ever heard speak on politics, or for that matter any other subject. He told the party opposed to him that their tongues were forked and that they lied with both forks. I thought then, and have not changed my opinion since that time, that a man with so much bitterness is unfit for office and more especially for congress where he had to represent not only his own people but all his constituents. Such strong prejudices should never possess a man who is the incumbent of an office and be elected by the people. In striking contrast with this man's bitterness I want to tell my readers about a politicial meeting I attended once in the city of Stockton, the fall of 1858. The first speech was by the candidate for Governor and it was noble and refined, not a word escaped his lips but what any one could listen to it vithout a blush on their cheeks. After him Charlie Fairfax came forth to address the people, and from his appearance he had been with the boys a little too long, but he soon steadied himself and begun. It seemed to be a time when some parties were anxious to unite with some others so as to carry the election successfully and Charlie wanted to illustrate that point and he did it in way of an anecdote. He said: "When I left Virginia to come to California I was engaged to be married to a very handsome young lady and as I was coming west I thought it best to release her from her obligation. I went to her house and had a very earnest talk with her and the contract was broken, but before it was broken off he said he made her promise three things. The first was that she should not marry a red-headed man, the second promise was that she should not marry a Scotchman and the third one was she should not marry a preacher. I came to California and made a very nice raise in the mines and went back home. It was very natural for me to want to see the young lady again. I rang the door bell and she came and ushered me into the parlor, but all this time she seemed to be very reserved. After awhile a red-headed child came crawling over the floor and I asked whose it was and she said it was hers. Well, who did you marry, and she said a red-headed Scotch preacher. That beats me and your promises both, for you have married all three in one."

There was a general burst of applause and the evening told in Fairfax's favor and he was elected by a very large majority. It is said while he was the clerk of the supreme court that he and an editor had trouble and the editor shot him in the neck and while the blood was pouring out on his assailant, for he had gained an advantage over him and had him pinned fast, he cocked his pistol over his heart and said, "were it not for you helpless family I would put a ball through you, but for their sake I am going to let you go," and arose and left him.

But I must return to the thread of my story after such a lengthy departure. During the spring of 1863 there was the survey of a ditch made running back into the mountains about twelve miles so as to divert some of the waters of Powder river and convey them down to Auburn for the use of those who had mining claims. The small gulches only supplied water for a short time in the spring and then were dry the remainder of the year. The latter part of June the owner of the projected ditch asked for help to build it. About forty men responded at first and others came on afterwards. With picks, shovels and blankets they made their way to the head of the ditch ready to begin work. In order to receive full pay each man was required to construct a given number of rods each day. All seemed to go to work with a good will, for most of them had mining claims and no water to work them. Everything went along smoothly until near the Fourth of July. Then some of the men wanted to go to Auburn and participate in an old fashioned

rousing jollification where they could get more grog
than they could in the mountains.   The boss told the
men on the third day that if they would stay and work
he would send to town and get plenty for them to drink
and they could have their sport in the wild woods.   He
knew, of course, that if he let them go to town and get
on a spree some of them would not come back and those
who did would not be in fit condition for work.   Almost
all the men remained and on the Fourth they were called
off two hours before the regular time and told, "There
is liquor and all who want it are welcome to it and must
help themselves."   It was not necessary to give the second invitation, nor was it long until a number of them
were jolly enough and were singing their Irish songs
and telling their Irish stories until the wild woods echoed
with their revelry.   With a number of others I was
seated talking about the day and how it used to be celebrated in a patriotic manner and in memory of the heroic
deeds of our forefathers.   Men would come to us and
say, "begorry, and why not take a little of the crater
and feel happy like ourselves."   Every once in awhile
one would take an eye opener and smack his lips as
though it was the best thing the Lord ever made for
man.   It was during the ribaldry and song and laughter
that a man who was a preacher whom I had never met
approached me and said, "I understand, sir, you are a
preacher."

I replied that I sometimes tried to preach, but made
no pretentions to being great or understanding all mysteries being only a common, plain, country parson and
I did not regard this as either a favorable time or place

to talk about religious matters.

"Oh, well," said he, "I wanted to ask you a plain, straight-forward question and it will not hurt you to answer it before these men "

I still contended that some other time would be much better even to ask a question, but as he was so persistant to ask it, and I would answer it as I thought best in view of the circumstances.

He proceeded, "Do you, sir, know all about the Bible which you are preaching?"

"No, sir, I do not. There are many mysteries in the Bible that I cannot understand and therefore cannot explain them."

"Then, sir," said he, "you ought never to enter the pulpit again or to try to preach to the people."

"Now," said I, " allow me if you please, to ask you a question?"

"Certainly, ask on."

"Do you know all about the Bible?"

By this time the boss and all the men who were sober enough were listening to see what the outcome would be.

"Yes, sir, I know all about the Bible and there are no mysteries in it, according to my way of thinking, that I cannot explain. Ask me any question you please and I will answer it."

"Well, sir, we read that 'Aaron made a golden calf at Sinar,' can you tell me whether it was a bull or a heifer?"

At that there was a general roar of laughter, and he replied, "the Bible does not tell me and I cannot tell you." Then he added, "you are the toughest case in the shape of a preacher I have ever found in all my travels." "Well," I replied "had you come to me at a proper time and in the right spirit I should have answered you quite differently, but you came boasting that you knew all about the Bible and trying besides to make out that I was grossly ignorant and I conclued the best plain was to answer a fool according to his folly."

After waiting a few moments he said, "I want to tell you what I do believe about the Bible."

"Very, well, sir, we will listen."

He then said, "I believe in the literal interpretation of the Scriptenes, that is taking them and believing in them all in a literal sense without any spiritual interpretation whatever, for God never intended it otherwise."

"Very well, sir, are you willing to stand by what you have just said."

"Certainly I am."

"Well, sir, I want you now to set a price on yourself, before these gentlemen as witnesses, for I want to buy you."

His reply was, "I am not for sale."

"That may be, but I do here and now insist on a price. I will pay anything you ask."

"What do you want with me?"

"You say you believe the Bible fully and want to take it as it reads. I want to make a mill site of you for the Bible says, 'He that believeth on me as the scriptures have said out of his belly shall flow rivers of living water.'"

Judge Myers of Santa Rosa, California, who was sitting by me and had been during the entire conversation said, "Parson, put him at the head of the ditch and we will soon be ready for mining down at Auburn."

Those near us became very much interested and they said, "Come, set your price; let us have it quick and we will soon make up money enough so the Parson can purchase you."

"Well, sir," he replied, "you are worse than ever, and such a preacher as you are I never saw before and never expect to see again."

Said I, "My friend let me give you a little advice, for I am a few years older than you. Never approach another stranger boasting about your knowledge of the Bible, and that its declarations must be taken literaly and that the one with whom you talk is ignorant."

As the men began to retire for the night I could hear them calling out to him, "Say, there, B., how much are you going to charge the Parson? We want this matter settled right away for then we will sleep better and have plenty of water for mining."

The next day those who worked near him were still quizzing him. The next morning he went to the boss and asked to be payed off, "for," said he, "I have made such a fool of myself I cannot have any more peace among the men." He left and I supposed found employment elsewhere. This sally was not all original for I have read of such things before.

CHAPTER XXIV.

While I lived in the Powder river mines my home was

about one fourth of a mile from town. One morning I went down quite early for my mail, which came in at night and sometimes quite late. As soon as I got to the village a friend of mine said, "Parson, we have very sad news this morning."

"What's the matter now?"

"Two young men were murdered last night in a saloon in the lower part of town."

"I will warrant," said I, "if mischief has been done and a crime committed it was in a saloon, for such places are the hot beds of crime."

These murders were not committed in the oldest "Mount of the Devil" but in one of the same kind established at a later date.

The victims were two young men who had just came from the Florence mines and it was said had brought considerable money with them and concluded they would sojourn for awhile at Powder river. They were from southern Oregon and their names were Larimore and Desmond. I suppose they were in the habit of playing cards and drinking some. At least they went to spend the evening in a saloon, the place which has been the ruin of so many young men. Both these young men were armed, one with a dirk and the other with a pistol. A small, dark-complexioned man, a greaser, came in near the same time and remarked, "Let us have a game of cards "

The three sat down at the card table and commenced playing and after they had played awhile (only betting for the drinks) one of the young men said to the other, "Let us quit for we are not in the habit of playing with men of his kind anyhow."

These remarks so enraged the Greaser that he quickly sprang to his feet, and as he got up the others stood up also and he grabbed the knife from Desmond's belt and stabbed him to the heart. He then snatched the pistol from Larimore's belt and shot him to death, both men dying at the card table before they could reach the door. During the excitement the murderer made his escape. In company with others I went down to the saloon. The two bodies lay on boards as bloody as they could well be, with the same clothing on in which they were killed, their regular mining suits. They had been in body fine specimens of men, weighing about 180 pounds each and were about thirty years old.

To me the scene was an exceedingly sad one and I could but think of the wretched work caused by the rum traffic. We found the saloon keeper still greatly excited, so that he scarcely knew what he was doing. He said, "I will starve before I will ever sell rum again."

He left the saloon just as it was and fled from the mines for fear he might be implicated also in the double murder. No one ever heard of the money said to belong to the two men. It was reported that the saloon keeper robbed them after their death but there was no certainty about the rumor.

At the time these murders were committed there was a regular county organization. The officers and miners agreed they would give $1000 for the arrest of the murderer. By some means there was a man who found his trail and followed him into Mormon basin, about twelve miles south of Auburn. He watched the movements of

the Spaniard very closely without letting anybody know
what his business was, and, of course, the murderer did
not suspect there was anyone watching him. Finally he
found where the Spaniard slept in the midst of some,
very thick brush and he went there and took his station
after the murderer had retired for the night and was
sound asleep He kept silent watch the remainder of
the night and when morning came the Spaniard sat up
in the bed, rubbing his eyes and not suspecting anything
wrong. When suddenly a voice, as of thunder, called
out to him, "Hold up your hands or then you are a dead
man."

He obeyed and his captor handcuffed him and then
tied him with a rope and with the assistance of another
man took him to Auburn. They were not molested on
the way and when they arrived the prisoner was delivered
over to the sheriff who fastened a chain to one leg.
That night a guard of sixty men was placed over him.
A meeting was called in the morning when the miners
decided not to wait for the regular term of court, as
there was no safe jail in which to keep him and it was
some time before the court would convene. Judges and
jurymen were soon appointed and the trial proceeded
rapidly. The criminal became suspicious that they
would mob him and had made arrangements with another
Spaniard to shoot him if the mob started with him. The
trial ended just before sunset, about the time I had entered the town and the verdict of the jury was guilty. I
saw a man run to a store and gather a coil of rope and
start with it to the place of trial, which was under a
large, open shed overlooking the town. The rope was

quickly arranged so as to form a running noose and the man lassoed like an unruly ox and twenty-six men quickly took hold of it and started down street at full run. The sheriff and his party tried to hold him but were soon overpowered.

As the mob started the Spaniard fired as he had promised, but missed his friend and shot a man by the name of Butler in the knee, crippling him for life. Some then started after the one who did the shooting and ran him several miles, but he being a very speedy footman outran them, making his escape and was never seen in those mines after that. In running with the murderer they sometimes had him head foremost and sometimes foot foremost. When they would strike a stump, and there were many of them, then he would be reversed and when they came in contact with another then he would change again. There was no shooting or noisy demonstrations as they proceeded but they ran rapidly about a quarter of a mile and then hung him to a limb. This was in the fall and when the judge came to hold court in the spring and learned of the affair he threatened to issue warrants for the arrest of every man who had hold of the rope. The miners soon had another meeting and informed the judge that if he carried out his threat his neck would be the next one to have a rope tightened around it. He concluded to let the matter pass without any further trouble or expense to the county.

CHAPTER XXV.

I propose now to tell the reader about the history of a man with whom I became well acquainted with in the mines, a fine scholar and a refined gentleman when at himself fully. He was born in what is known as the blue grass region of Kentucky, a place famous for its nutritous grasses and the excellent quality of its beef and the hospitality of its inhabitants as well as their thrift. In a lovely portion of that region there stood a fine brick mansion, just outside of a prosperous town, containing one of the oldest colleges in the state. The house was surrounded by a gentle sloping lawn of blue grass with beautiful gravel walks on all sides and these walks had fine shrubery and flowers along their borders. There were numerous shade trees in the front yard arranged with nice seats under them which were delightful on a warm summer's day. Back of the house was the barn and still back of it was the farm and pasture lands, all sloping to the west. The mansion was neatly painted and penciled and being on an elevated piece of ground it presented a very handsome appearance to those who traveled the county road in front of it. A very happy family dwelt here, the father being an honored elder in the Cumberland Presbyterian church and one who "worshiped God with all of his house." The mother had decended from a noble family, who had taken a leading part in the revolutionary war, as well as in the war of 1812. This esteemed couple had an abundance of the world's goods and were ever ready with both heart and hand to assist the worthy poor and do good as they had opportunity. They were regular attendants on religious worship in the town and gave liberally of their means to support it. In fact, they were the main supports of their pastor in carrying on the work of the church. There was a prosperous college in the town, founded and carried on by the same religious denomination of which they were members, and Mr. Miller was one of its trustees and main supports financially. Many young men have been educated there who were useful as ministers and many more have gone forth as politicial leaders in the state. Our own state of California was blessed in its earlier history by the good influence of one who graduated from that school and was at the time of his death at the head of a theological seminary. It was in the midst of these nice surroundings and in the beautiful mansion on the hill that the hero of my story, a Mr. Miller, had his birth and was reared to manhood.

If a beautiful spot of earth and noble parentage could make men useful and refined, then Mr. M. ought to have shone as a star of the first magnitude and have been one of the very best of men. He attended the district school until he was old enough and far enough advanced to enter college. After entering college, being naturally possessed of a brilliant mind, he made very rapid advancement and was a great favorite of the professors and of his schoolmates and the community generally. His conduct was exemplary and his parents and friends had great hopes that his future would be bright and his sunset without a single cloud to overshadow it. At last the day of his graduation came and he stood at the head of his class honored and respected by all. His mother's

heart bounded for joy when she saw the position he had
nobly earned and hoped he would be a strong prop on
whom she could lean for her support in her declining
days.

Near the time of his graduation there was a lovely
young lady who graduated from the same school.   She
too was of an excellent family and a leader among her
schoolmates and a bright scholar as well as one greatly
admired by all who knew her.   Mr. M. had been acquainted with her from childhood, for she had lived on a
farm with her parents near where he resided.   When
children they had gambled over the blue grass meadows
together enjoying their innocent childhood sports.

He made proposals of marriage to her and was accepted.   The day for the ceremony was set, and at the
appointed hour a happy company assembled and spoke
of the marriage as an excellent one.   The minister, who
had long been their pastor, spoke the solemn words
which made them husband and wife.   His father gave
them a good farm with a neat cottage on it, where they
lived as happy and contented as heart could wish.   Not
a single shadow had as yet crossed their threshold and
to them was born a lovely child who was the joy of their
lives.

Adjoining their farm lived a man who had always
proved to be a very troublesome neighbor and delighted
in quarreling and back biting   Nothing seemed to please
him better than to see one neighbor arrayed against another and if it proved to be a deadly conflict it seemed
to suit him all the better.   His friends were few, if any,

and the community would have preferred that he move into some howling wilderness for a home. He was cross and morose and with it all very overbearing in his disposition. He was very poor and jealous of the prosperity of the rich above him. In fact a more unhappy, disagreeable man would be hard to find even within prison walls. He was a most wretched man and in disposition was ugly in the extreme. He had imposed on Mr. M. until forbearance ceased to be a virtue. One day these neighbors met and the one who ''neither feared God nor regared man" commenced a tirade of abuse, calling the peaceable one all manner of names and finally made as though he would do him bodily harm but when he drew near enough, the man who was so unjustly assailed struck him, killing him almost instantly. He then went to town and told the authorities what he had done. He was placed under arrest although many thought he ought to go free.

At the preliminary examination he was bound over to appear in a higher court, his father and brother going on his bonds for $4000. He was afraid to risk the consequences of remaining for fear he might have to spend a term in state's prison. He and his wife talked the matter over very seriously and as he had often spoken about going to California they concluded he had better go before the court met. Railroads had not been built to any extent in Kentucky at the time. When he departed he left his wife in tears, wishing the difficulty had never occurred She bid him farewell with the injunction, "To live in the future so that he would be as much respected as in the past, for it was purely an unintentional act on his part."

He made his way to New York City where he soon
found a steamer ready to sail for the Golden West. He
purchased a ticket and at the proper time went aboard
and was soon out on the great ocean, tossed by its ever
restless waves, which he acknowledged were good
emblems of the restless spirit dwelling in him

The voyage proved to be a very successful one and in
due time he arrived in San Francisco. He did not tarry
long there but purchased a mining outfit and made his
way into the mountains. He soon secured an excellent
mining claim and went to work with a determined will.
It was not long until he had accumulated quite a fortune
and sent the money back to his father and brother for
going on his bonds and also to pay his wife's expenses to
California.

The portion of the state where he mined there was a
scarcity of water for mining purposes but some very rich
diggings and with some others he ventured into the survey of a ditch which was to reach back into the mountains a number of miles. After the survey the ditch was
built, he being the largest shareholder. They expected
the coming season to reap a golden harvest from their
investments as well as in the years to come. That winter
proved to be a very hard one for heavy rains and winds
and the ditch and flumes which had been completed
before the winter had set in were almost completely demolished.

Before the destruction of his hopes his wife arrived
in San Francisco and accompanied him to his mountain
home. When she came to her new residence she found

neither church nor sabbath school, but found Sunday a
day of drinking, gambling and terrible carousing— scenes
she had never witnessed before. She endured these
hardships of the sabbath day a little while and then began to long for the home of her childhood with its quiet
Sundays and times of rest. Her husband soon discovered
her great dissatisfaction and how unhappy she was getting to be and knew very well the cause of it, when he
said to her, "I will furnish you with $5000 and pay your
expenses back home if you wish to go."

It was mutually agreed that it would be the best for
her to go where she could educate their child and raise
him in good society. He went with her to the city and
saw her safely aboard the vessel with their lovely little
boy. Farewell caresses and blessings were exchanged
and she turned her face towards her old Kentucky home
and he toward his mountain dwelling.

He sold his mining claim and devoted his entire energies to his ditch, for he was elected superintendent. It
was the winter after his wife left which proved so dis-
astrous to the investment he had made. He saw the
raging floods tear away a great deal of the banks from
his ditch and the heavy winds blow down his flumes and
tressle works, in fact he saw the entire ruin, financially,
of his company.

From that time on he did not prove the hero he had
been in former days, but his courage seemed to forsake
him utterly and he let matters drift along very carelessly.
Finally in his time of weakness and want of courage he
could be seen occasionally about saloons, not drinking
at first but only looking on as a mere spectator. Before

this he had stood aloft from such places, knowing the evil found there, but now he commenced by little to yield and would take a dram occasionally to drown his sorrows. He had a little money left from his financial wreck and the rum power knew it and they determined to secure it at all hazards. At the time he wanted moral support the most he found himself surrounded by all that was profane and immoral and that only tended to his speedier downfall and utter ruin. He drank heavily for several years, until, from a strong robust man with great strength, he was reduced to a mere skeleton.

Finally some of his friends who had known him in his prosperous days proposed to help him if he would go with them to the Powder river mines, for he had now spent all his money and was living on charity such as it was. They hoped when he would get away from his old associates and get where there was no liquor sold he would reform and be a stalwart man again and trample his enemy under his feet and stand erect as a man among men. Between California and the mines there were no saloons and, of course, he could not drink only as some one would give it to him. As soon as he arrived in the mines he saw the signifficent sign "Mount Diabolo," and with all the warning given from that sign he made his way thither and had an "eye opener."

It was in these mines that I made his acquaintance and under rather peculiar circumstances. A man had erected a two story building, and the lower portion he used for a dwelling and a saloon. The front part was occupied with the saloon and the back portion for the dwelling. The upper story was used as a hall in which church and court was both held.   I had the use of this hall Sabbaths in which to preach.   At the close of the services the first Sunday I occupied it, the saloon keeper and his wife invited me to dine with them, and, as I was "batching" I gladly accepted the invitation.   It was during this meal time that I formed the acquaintance of this Mr. Miller and observed his gentlemanly bearing.   The owner of the saloon sat opposite to me at the table and remarked, "that he must be in something of a hurry today as he had to attend bar while his bartender came to dinner." He soon finished his meal and excused himself.

A few moments after he passed out a fine looking man with gentlemanly bearing came in.   He was tall and erect, showing by his movements that he had been well raised, although is was plainly to be seen that he was drinking.   Is it not very singular how soon liquor begins to show itself on the drinker's nose and that he soon carries about with him a mark as distinct as Cain's.

After the lady of the house had introduced us and retired, he said: "Parson I have not always been as you see me today, selling whiskey and not only selling it but drinking it, but once I was a regular attendant at church and enjoyed its servives.   In an evil hour I gave way and my constitution is ruined by strong drink to such an extent that I am no longer able to do hard work.   If I could obtain a situation where I would not have to labor very hard I would quit this business at once and forever, for I know it is wrong to sell that which has proven my ruin as well as the ruin of thousands."

He still continued the conversation and said: "There

was a time in California when I considered myself to be worth between $80,000 and $100,000 and I invested the larger share of it in a mining ditch and flumes, which were ruined by the winter's storms and I was, to use a miner's phrase, "broke."

He told me he gaduated from a college near his father's home and that he married as nice a young lady as ever graduated from any school. "But," said he, as the tears filled his eyes, "I have disgraced it all and I am a moral wreck and a wretched drunkard, allowing my appetite to control me. By my drinking I have brought disgrace, not only on my parents and old friends, but also on her whom I swore at the altar to protect and defend, as well as on my darling boy. They are back at the old home and I am glad of it, while I am here a poor, miserable man almost ready to die."

I asked him if he had not courage and manhood enough left to reform and be a useful man.

"No," said he, "never as long as I have to sell liquor to earn my bread and butter. If any one had told me I would ever get so low as to stand behind a bar and sell liquor in the room below, while a minister was preaching in the room above, I never would have believed it fifteen years ago, but such is the fact today.

He continued as bartender at that saloon for some time, but finally got to drinking so much that he was dismissed. His money was soon gone and he obtained his meals, at least the most of them, by begging them from the miners. He went into Powder river valley and lived for a time among a farming community. I was away from the camp for some time and did not know

what had become of him. One day in November I met
him in the road, but he had changed so much I scarcely
knew him. He was so weak that it was with great difficulty that he could walk. He said he was broke and
did not know what would become of him; he supposed
some one would bury him when he died and that was
not going to be long. With the very deepest emotion,
hearing his bosom, he cried out, "Oh, Parson, can you
not do something for a poor, unfortunate wretch like
me."

He was going towards town and I was going from
it. I told him to go on and when I returned I would
see what could be done for him. When I came back I
went to see a family whom I had known from my boy-
hood days, and it so happened that the husband had
known the father of the unfortunate man in Kentucky.
I soon made arrangements with them to care for him
while he lived, which at the farthest would only be a few
days, and I would make the best effort I could to rsise
money to pay them for their trouble, agreeing, if I could
secure the money, they should have at least $3 a day for
their trouble. I assisted him to his new home, which
was with Rev. N. Johnson's family, the man who
thought to add "fifteen years to his life by going to
Oregon."

He seemed very grateful for what I had done and
very penitent for the life he had led. One day I visited
him late in the afternoon and saw that he was very near
his eternal home, and concluded the best time to get
money for him was while he was yet alive. I went to
town (which was about a half mile away) as soon as I

could and drew up a subscription paper and visited all
the stores and saloons. I soon had money sufficient to
pay for taking care of him and to bury him decently,
but in a very plain manner as all who died in the mines
were. While I was visiting the last saloon in search of
money a gentleman came in and said he had just died
and that it would be necessary to bury him the next day.
He died from consumption and rotten whiskey and although the weather was cool is was thought best to bury
him quickly, for it was even difficult for the family to remain in the room where he was laid out, and houses
there had but one room as a rule. It might be said that
families were only camping and expected to move on in
the spring.

In the spring this family left and I have never seen
them since. The next day it was snowing and blowing
and very cold, it being about the middle of November,
1863. The coffin and grave were ready about 4 o'clock
and his remains were borne to their last resting place by
the hands of his friends. The grave was on a rising
piece of ground about one-fourth of a mile southeast of
Auburn. There we left him in the care of one who
watches over our dust till he shall bid it rise. This was
the closing scene in the career of one naturally bright
and intelligent and who had at times noble impulses but
gave way in the hour of temptation and went on down,
down, until at last he filled a drunkard's grave and had
to be laid away by strange hands. What I have related
in the forgoing story is the truth for after his death his
papers were examined and many of the facts here related
concerning him were learned through them   These

papers were forwarded to his old home in the east, together with the account of his last days and of his
burial.

CHAPTER XXVI.

In June, 1864, I concluded to bid the mines farewell
and return to my California home, having been absent
more than two years. There were three of us who left
Powder river on horseback. We crossed Burnt river at
the old emigrant road where I had crossed in 1851. We
followed up this road until we came to one turning to
the right, just above a very hot spring a few hundred
yards from our road, and going on this road it led us
into the gold and silver mines of Owyhee. Near these
hot springs we saw where the lightning had struck an
ox team and instantly killed three out of four of them.
They were left in their tracks, a great scare-crow for
horses.

After passing beyond this spring and partly round it
we commenced to ascend a very high hill, in fact it
might be called a mountain for it was the dividing ridge
between two rivers. On the summit of this ridge we
met two men on horseback, when one of them said,
"How are you, Parson? I am glad to see you for I have
been owing you a bill for more than a year and I want to
pay it. I was afraid you would leave this part of the
country without me seeing you at all."

"You must be mistaken," I replied.

"No," said he, "I am not, for you married me and I
have never paid you for it. Come, get down and let me

rid my conscience of that debt. I have nothing but gold
dust but will try to pour you out enough, as we have no
means of weighing it."

He intended giving me $30 but when weighed it proved
to be $28. After the usual farewells and good wishes
(for even miners are sometimes polite) we journeyed on
and spent the night with friends in the Ohywee mines.
Here we found a man with a two-horse team going directly to Placerville in California and he did not want to
travel alone for the Indians had been troublesome near
that road only a short time prior to this. It was not
long until we made a bargain with him and I disposed
of my riding animal and saddle.

The country we passed over after leaving the Ohywee
was a very high rolling one with a scarcity of both water
and timber. The land seemed rich enough for it was
covered with an excellent growth of grass. In our travels
we found what had once been a forest of pine but it had
been consumed by fire, except some stumps and these
we found were petrified. At that time there were only
a few houses in Paradise valley and they looked lone-
some, but I suppose ere this the country is settled and
Uncle Sam has them under his protecting wing and they
are hoping for the time to come when silver will be on a
par with gold and the country not ruled so much by
gold bugs. During our journey we crossed the Humboldt mountains and while on the summit we witnessed
one of the grandest scenes of terror I ever gazed upon.
I had passed through some of these storms of thunder
and lightning on Platte river in crossing the plains and
at the time never expected to see anything worse, it

mattered not where my steps might tend   But this on
Humboldt seemed to be a concentration of many storms
and all pouring forth their fury at once and in a very
small compass.   We had just passed over the summit of
the Humboldt mountains and commenced going down a
dry ravine when a small cloud came floating along
charged very heavily with electricity and rolling thunder.
Soon the lightning began to play and the loud thunders
rolled until the earth trembled and all our wagons tires
were a sheet of electric flame.   We had our firearms in
the wagon and all thought it very doubtful whether we
would come out alive and every moment we expected to
see the horses struck with the electric darts which were
shooting all around us.   While these scenes of terror
were being displayed before our eyes it commenced to
rain.   Did I say commenced to rain? Yes, it commenced
to pour.   How can I describe it truthfully for it seemed
like we were all going to be drowned as we traveled on,
and even after we had taken shelter behind an abobe
building, which was fast melting away, it seemed no
better.   The only idea that I can give of that storm is to
say that the little cloud which came floating over us was
like a cistern, a fourth of a mile in diameter and the
same in height, filled with water to the brim when all at
once the bottom fell out and that immense body of water
all came down at once.   In a few moments our once dry
gulch was a raging torrent, at least thirty feet wide, but
we had taken refuge behind an adobe saloon which was
located on the ground above the torrent that went rushing past us.   The saloon keeper saw his saloon building
melting away like wax before a blazing fire and he stood

and cursed his maker for sending a storm that had ruined his business and broken his bottles of rum. Below the house, perhaps a hundred and fifty yards, the hills closed in forming a wall on each side of the creek while the only road through that mountain gorge was down this stream which had so lately been nothing but a dry gulch. Had we entered that canyon just before that storm we would have lost our wagon and team if not our own lives, for the waters rose fifteen or twenty feet in height leaving its mark on the rocky walls. The flood rolled large rocks out on to the Humboldt flat that must have weighed several tons. There was a man who kept a hotel about one and a half miles below us and he had planted a garden, which, he said, had came up and was growing finely, but the storm had swept garden and soil into the river leaving him the rocks on which to plant another garden.

I was in the signal service office at Washington city in 1873 and spoke of this storm and old "probabilities" told me that it was the second time that wagon tires blazed with electricity and the occupants of the wagon spared so far as reported to them.

We passed through Virginia and Carson cities and went over the mountains on the Placerville road. Near the summit of the Sierra Nevadas we met the stage running on a bet of $10,000 against the Dutch Fat stage. It was expected this drive would settle the route of the Central Pacific railroad. The Placerville stage beat the other several hours and when we met them they had four horses, two drivers and no passengers. They killed several horses on the trip but it is well known that Dutch

Flat got the road.

In connection with this wonderful display of nature I want, before I close this chapter, to speak of some other scenes that I have witnessed on this coast. A few years ago we were on our way home, after attending church in the city of Petaluma, one beautiful Sabbath day. We had gained the summit of a small hill near where Mr. Seymour lives, when we witnessed, not a scene of terror, but one of beauty such as I never expect to see again. Beyond us, but near enough to be in plain view was the commencement of the waters of the great ocean, as blue and beautiful as anyone ever saw them. The waters covered an expanse east and west and north of us as far as the eye could reach. Not only were the waters blue but their borders carpeted with green grass which added to the beauty of the scene before us Out in the direction of Stony Point vessels could be seen with sails all spread to catch the winds which at the time were blowing very gently. They seemed to be moving very quietly before the breeze. In the midst of this vast expanse of water large rocks reared their massive heads far above the surface and the breakers were rolling and tumbling and throwing their foam high in the air. There was not a tree or a shrub of the many groves belonging to Mr. Mecham to be seen, but all in that direction was the blue ocean with its rocks, vessels and breakers. Any one who has traveled up the coast has seen scenes such as I have just described if he was near enough the borders of the ocean to look on it, but this was the first time I ever saw the ocean pictured on dry ground. Some of my readers may conclude that what I have here described

are only the imaginings of some old crank who wants to
give something new for the world to think about.   I
know what I saw and there were two women and two
children who saw the same scenes.   I once had a talk
with a sea captain, who had sailed in Alaska waters, and
he told me that he had often seen large cities with their
cathedrals and churches and immense business blocks
pictured when they were thousands of miles from any
city.   How such pictures are made I shall not attempt
to tell but will leave that to men of scientific pursuits
and attainments.   Those who have crossed the plains to
this portion of our country will remember the lakes they
thought they saw on ahead and when they advanced
found nothing but an alkali desert.   I remember once
in 1858 going from Stockton to San Ramos valley in
Contra Costa county in my buggy.   After crossing the
San Joaquin river and advancing a mile or more on the
plains I looked ahead, and, as I thought, saw a band of
armed men coming.   At the time there were places in
California where the rougher element of the Spanish
race was very troublesome to travelers and of course my
mind caught on that thought first.   There was no chance
to back out for they would overtake me before I could
recross the river on the ferry boat.   There was no house
in sight on that side and it was twelve miles ahead to the
first dwelling.   All I could do was to press on and risk
the consequences.   Sometimes when people are frightened they say their hearts are in their mouths, and if
anything of the kind ever did take place it did with me
that morning.   But on I went, although my heart beat
fast, and when I came up to them I found a band of

Spanish cattle that had been on the plains feeding and were then going to the river for water. Spanish cattle then were sometimes as bad as Spanish men for they frequently chased those who rode in buggies for miles. I felt very much relieved when the cattle passed me without interruption. There seemed to be at least two kinds of mirage, one which throws its pictures on land, while the other lifts objects up and presents them in a very unnatural position. The one I saw near Petaluma was of the first kind and by far, I think, the most beautiful. This picture will never be erased from my mind while I live.

CHAPTER XXVII.

Well, here we are, back in California again, and glad of it for it is the largest state in the union for its size. Has the largest trees in the world and immense water falls. Large canals for irrigating purposes and large colleges in which to educate the youth of our land. Large mountains and large men of large brain and large enterprise. Large, fine-looking women and handsome children. It is large and generous in climate, large in fruits and oranges, and, as a rule, large-hearted people live within its borders. It is large and has been for many years in the number that needed it and ought to be hung. It is large in its public schools and its qualifications for teaching. It has large cathedrals and churches, large ministers who get wise above what is written, that is a few of them. They even make large assertions and deny a portion of the old Bible which has proved a firm foundation for nations as well as individuals. Not only these things but we have very large saloons and very large drinkers who look like bloated swill tubs. We have large cattle and large hogs and large horses. Some men do business in such a large way that the overflow is too much for them and they ruin themselves financially.

But in the midst of this country of large things there is a large amount of moral and religious work to be done and let us look around a little as we are now back home and see what we can do to help these things along. One man says, "Parson are you not discouraged to see such slow progress?"

By no means; if the cause is God's men may do their best against the Bible and against the cause it advocates and they will stand firmer than the mountains which are our eastern boundray. It took omnipotence quite a while to make a world and then make it as beautiful as it is with fruits and trees and flowers. It was many a century after the promise of a Savior until he came to make known God's will to man and to make atonement for our last race. It will take time to redeem the world and cause it to cry out, "The Lord God omniportent reigneth."

But it is coming just as sure as God lives for he has promised it in his word, "For all shall know me, from the least to the greatest." Let us then look around and see where we can bear a little part in bettering the world's condition. Here it is the church says, "We want you to be our missionary agent or superintendent in the bonds of the Pacific Synod and go forth and preach the gospel and be instrumental in setting idle hands to work and strengthening those who are already trying to advance the Master's kingdom."

Let us then begin the work by going over first to the south side of the Stanislaus river with a brother to assist in the preaching. The place was known as the Fagan school house. Then the country was but sparsely settled and the inhabitants esteemed it a great privilege to come together for worship and for a social time. But even in such communities as this sometimes differences arise and they need the gracious outpouring of the Holy Spirit to set them right again. A minister had been preaching there for a few months, when, by some means, one of the elders became offended and he and the minister were having trouble, and as each one had his friends it caused a division in the neighborhood. When we arrived we heard of the difficulty and resolved as the first effort of the meeting to see if it could not be settled, knowing that no religious effort could prosper while the main members and leaders were having trouble. A meeting of the two contending parties and an elder was called and after prayer each one was called on for a statement. When this was given it was soon found that the trouble was not of a very serious nature, at least not so serious but what the parties could be reconciled if they would show the true forgiving spirit of Christians. It was something of a struggle, for human nature does not like to yield and it is only the divine within us that causes us to forgive our brother his trespasses. At last love conquered and tears flowed as they gave each other the right hand of fellowship. When we met in the public congregation that night the actions of these two

brethern showed plainly they had been reconciled for
they entered into the services of the hour with a hearty
good will. Not only the people of God but men of the
world said, "After all there is something in the church
which we have not experienced or then troubles could
not be settled as readily as that had been." If the church
wants a revival of religion the first thing to be done is to
get trouble out of the way if there is any. Settlement
of difficulties is a good revival of itself. We are first to
be reconciled to our brother and then offer the gift and
the Lord will hear.

The sermon on Sabbath was on the sixth of Romans,
"Therefore being buried with Christ by baptism into
death; that like as Christ was raised from the dead by
the glory of the Father, even so we also should walk in
newness of life." The main theme was the new birth or
being born again showing that in regeneration we are
buried with Christ and as he became invisible to his old
character after the work of regeneration by the Holy
Spirit. As Christ had new life when he arose, so the
believer arises to a new life in Christ. He is dead to his
old character of sin but lives by the power of him who
raised Christ from the dead. The effort was to show
that this chapter did not refer to any outward ordinance,
such as water baptism, but to the baptism which is purely spiritual. That no outward forms could by any
possibility save us, that the Holy Spirit alone renews the
soul and prepares us for heaven. This plain and pointed
preaching told on those who heard any many through
that holy Sabbath day resolved to lead a better life.

There was an appointment for Monday with the request that seekers of religion be present with all others who desired to come. There were quite a number who attended and after the reading of the scripture and prayer those who wished special instructions in the way of salvation were requested to occupy a certain seat. There was no need of a second invitation for every non-professor in the room came forward for prayers and instruction. Among the number who came forward was a young man or rather one middle-aged who said, "I have been a seeker of religion the past twenty years and I have never found the Savior yet."

The instructions given were of the plainest kind so that all could understand it. It was soon very evident that the man of whom I speak, his name was Moore, was very near the kingdom and would soon enter, receiving the baptism of the Holy Spirit. As we passed on, giving instructions to others, he rose to his feet and said, "I want to make a confession I never made in my life. God for Christ's sake has pardoned my sins." This new born soul, like all who are born again, desired the salvation of others and he was soon found telling others how to be saved and it was only a short time until all who came forward for prayers were rejoicing with our friend in God's pardoning love. It was a glad hour for all who were present and all who could sing were singing, "I have just received the bounty with glory in my soul;" "Heaven came down our souls to greet and glory crowned the mercy seat." Happy company much like heaven itself.

Mr. Moore, who first found Christ that day, was in rather poor health and not long after this he began to decline very rapidly. It was not more than a year after this that it was plainly to be seen his mind was affected and it was not long until he was entirely deranged and had to be taken to the asylum at Stockton. He forgot the name of his parents, of his brothers and sisters and his old neigbors and even his own name he did not remember, but to the very last hours of his life there was one thing he did not forget and that was, "God had power on earth to forgive sins and that he loved his Saviour." He could tell when and where he was saved and could talk about the meeting on Monday in the school house. On this subject he seemed clear and rational but on all other things his mind was a blank. He could not name those who were present at the meeting but he knew he was there and that his sins were pardoned and joy and gladness filled his soul. He died a very triumphant death praising God as long as he had strength.

After this meeting I went over to Merced and held a meeting in Merced City and in a school house several miles below town. The elder here told me that ministers had been preaching there that men could "get religion," as they termed it, and then lose it again as often as they saw proper. He asked me to present the real Bible view on that subject and I promised to do so. I used as a text "Heb. 6-19. Which hope we save as an anchor of the soul both sure and steadfast, and which entereth into that within the vail; whether the forrunner is for us entered even Jesus." I never intimated but what all the world believed when God saved and regenerated a soul hat it was a work that lasted forever. That the anchor

would hold amid the worst storms because it was sure
and steadfast and fastened in Christ the forrunner who
was within the vial. I argued that God was such a perfect workman that he did not need and had no occasion
to repeat himself; that when he made the world he did
not have to make it over on account of the work being
deficient. Being born again was a purely spiritual work
wrought by the Holy Spirit in the heart and as it was
God's work it did not and would not have to be done
over. I presented God's promises that it would never
leave nor forsake us and before I had closed the sermon
a good Methodist sister rose to her feet, shouting, telling
the neighbors they had "heard God's truth and that it
must and would do good."

While on the Merced river I formed the acquaintance
of an old pioneer and he told me about some of the early
days in that portion of the state. He said the time was
when it was almost impossible to keep hogs, cattle or
horses. There were a great many greasers, a mixture of
Spanish and Indian, and the larger number of them
would steal whenever they could. He said, "The citizens, what few they were, had to organize for self protection or then leave the country." Whenever they found
one of these greasers had stolen stock in his possession
they either shot him down in his tracks or left him
swinging to the limb of a tree as a warning to others.
He said he chased and shot them down with just as
little compunctions of conscience as he ever did a prarie
wolf or a sheep-killing dog. It may be thought this was
extremely rough treatment and so it was, but it became
necessary in order to save life and property It is nat-

ural for a man to defend his rights and protect himself
and family from harm when in his power. It was the
only way to keep property and open up the country to
a desirable class of citizens. A greaser who behaved
himself as he ought was safe from these vigilance com-
mittees but woe be to him if he was found with stolen
property in his possession. There have been times in
California when the people had to take the law in their
own hands and administer justice and when it had been
done good results frequently followed. It is, however,
a bad state of society when such measures have to be
resorted to but when it is done scoundrels dread it more
than they do the courts and juries. There ought to be a
high regard and a deep respect for the courts, but if they
do wrong and clear one criminal after another who
ought to be in state's prison or hung for his crimes or
then delay the hanging year after year then the patience
of the people become exhausted and they look out for
their own interests. With a great many of the rougher
element from almost every nation under heaven it is a
great wonder that the people of this state have not much
oftener taken the law into their own hands, but we are
glad that the society of this state is as good as it is and I
can see improvement more or less every year.

Human life is more sacred than it used to be and so
are the rights of property. Drinking is not as respect-
able as it used to be but there is still abundant evidence
that man is a sinner and that his nature must be changed
before he is prepared to dwell where there is no sin to be
found. Advancing in morals is very slow work but as
long as it keeps moving along encouragment should be
given.

CHAPTER XXVIII.

1 was living once on a public road leading into the city of Santa Rosa. The road at that time had never been worked to good advantage and in the winter time it was in a very bad condition, especially after a rain storm. Extending from where we lived towards town for at least a few hundred yards had never been graveled and there were some low places in it. These low places were sometimes a foot in depth and very miry on account of constant travel, and wagons frequently stuck fast and had to be helped out. One morning a wagon loaded with fish came along just as we were going out to the barn to milk and the driver was swearing terribly at his horses so as to help them pull the wagon through the mud. 1 said to my companion, "That man ought to stick fast in the mud for using such ugly language as that." The words were not much more than out of my mouth when sure enough the wagon was fast in the mud and his team could not pull it out.

Just as we finished milking he came for help. I told him I would assist him on one condition. "Well," said he, "name it quick, for I ought to be in town selling my fish."

I told him the condition was that he was never to swear in passing my place and not to swear a single oath while I helped him out of the mud hole.

"Come on," said he, "it is all right 1 will do that much."

When we came to his wagon we took all the fish out for they were in baskets and carried them across the mud hole and then took some rails and raised the wheels.

I took hold of the lines and commanded the horses to go, but no, they were stalled and discouraged and very poor. Finally I told him he had better drive his own team as he was used to them. He took hold of the lines and urged them to go, but not a pound would they pull. He stood still for a few moments and seemed to be in a very serious study for he knew he was losing the early sale of his fish. Finally, with sorrow depicted in his countenance, while he looked at me very intently and with a smile, said, "See, here, Mister, you have got to let me swear once or we will never get out of this mud hole."

"No, sir," said I, "I shall not give you any such privilege. You know what you promised and if you violate your word it is at your own risk and not my fault."

"Well," said he, "whether you consent to it or not I must swear," and he uttered a tremendous oath, when the team took the wagon out with but little effort. After he was out of his difficulty and the fish were placed in the wagon again, he asked, "How much do I owe you, sir."

I told him I never charged a man anything for helping him out of a difficulty like that.

"You have earned something working in this mud and here are two rock cod for your breakfast."

I thanked him and he drove on to town and although he passed frequently after this I never heard him swear any more. He told me afterwards that morning's work made him think more about the sinfullness of swearing and the folly of using an oath at all than anything that had ever happened to him. He said his team pulled better without swearing than they ever did with it. Some men seem to think that others will not consider them as being in earnest unless they clinch it with an oath strong enough to make one shudder to hear it. If a man tells me of some incident with which he was familiar and then closes his story with an oath so as to fasten it tight, as he supposes, I begin at once to doubt whether he has told me the truth about it. Some men say, ''I swear and do not know it.'' If this is true you must have indulged in the habit for a long time. Bad habits should cease immediately for they are neither good manners nor good sense.

I was once traveling with a number of men on horseback and among them was a man who was swearing terribly and every little while calling on God to damn his soul. Finally I said to him, "Why not stop swearing by your Creator and swear by your own father whom you serve so faithfully."

''Who is my father,'' said he.

I told him the devil was and that he was employed by him to do his dirty ugly work. God never taught you to swear.

He said, "I wonder how that would work," and then he commenced to use the name of the devil in the place of God, his maker. The swearing was so awkward that the entire company roared with laughter; but such was his habit he kept on in the old style. I have heard some men swear when it did not seem so rough as it did with others.

I remember a good-natured Irishman who came to my

house one day with potatoes for sale. At that time he
only delivered one sack and promised the other before
long.   How often after that he passed to Santa Rosa with
potatoes I do not know but one thing I do know, he
failed to bring me a sack at all that year. The next
season, after he had raised another crop, and I had almost forgotten the transaction, I looked towards the
front gate one day and saw a man advancing toward me
with a sack on his back, when he called out, "Hay, there
mister, did you think I was going to hell wid a sack of
spuds on my back."

I confess I had to laugh at the wit of Paddy for once,
even if he was a little profane.   Poor fellow, he dropped
dead from his horse a few years ago and his faithful
beast remained by him all night, and it and his dogs
kept faithful watch over him.

Now, I want to speak of another California incident in
which I was badly plagued by the quick wit of a woman.
Almost forty years ago there lived in a California town
an agent of the California Steam Navigation Company
who was known to be very abusive and overbearing with
many who had dealings with him.   If things did not go
to suit him he would swear terribly.   Many people had
often wished that something would happen to him that
would make him more humble and obliging to the pat-
rons of the company.   It is a singular fact that a little
brief authority puffs some men up with pride to such an
extent that they think common people are far beneath
their notice.   I have seen politicians who before election
were all smiles and pleasantness, but when the contest
was over and they were elected to some office, even that of

squire or constable, would feel so large that they seemed to think it was a great condesension to speak to men of moderate means who had cast their ballots for them, such should never hold any office whatever. I could give instances where men were elected and it caused them to swell "to utter bursting nigh" to such an extent that they were loathed by their best friends. How often we hear the remark made of such men, "What a pity tis for a young man of fine promise to ruin himself with his disguisting bigotry. I voted for him but I will never do it again.

The agent of whom I speak seemed to be one of the men who thought he must have a large share of bighead just because he was the employe of a rich corporation. If he was a shareholder in the concern I never heard of it and even if he was that did not authorize him to act ugly with those who had business to transact with him.

One day a hardy miner came down from the mountains where he had been mining and had some business at the office, when the agent, as usual, commenced his abuse. The miner looked on him with mild but earnest eyes for a time and then told him firmly that where he lived and where he had been raised such language was not allowed. That it was not the remarks of a gentleman and he must quit it.

The agent replied very sharply, "That he was in the habit of doing as he pleased without the advice of any one."

The hardy miner warned him not to repeat his insults and that if he did he would give him a thrashing such as he would remember many days. He soon repeated his insults, when the miner did as he said he would, punishing the fellow so severely that it was difficult for him to attend to his duties as agent for several days. The authorities of the town were so glad of it that the man was not arrested, nor a fine imposed, but said they hoped it would be a lesson to the agent as long as he lived. It was said that it wrought such a change with the agent that afterwards he was gentlemanly and polite to all who had dealings with him.

Not long after this I was at the house of a friend in company with a number of men who had called, when the conversation turned toward the navigation company and how they were displeasing the public and if they kept on the result would be the organization of another company. I remarked that at our town we had one of their agents who was abusive and insulting and that a miner came down from the mountains the other day and thrashed him severely and I thought if he had another such drubbing he might become a better man and learn to treat people as he ought. The lady of the house, who was and elderly woman and very shrewd and witty, had nothing to say on the subject until I closed my remarks in reference to the agent, when she raised her hand and pointing her finger at me said, ''Go home, sir, and thrash him. The Lord made you and called you to do all the good you could and if you can do good by thrashing him, you certainly ought to do it. Go home, sir, and do you duty.''

All present roared with laughter at my expense and I acknowledged I was badly beaten by one woman at least.

Everybody who knew this woman loved to be in her company. She always had a cheerful word for all about her and was regarded always as an excellent christian. She dearly loved children and they were always pleased when they could be in her company.

I was superintendent of the Home Mission work in the Pacific synod for two years and during that time there was more than 200 accessions to the church at the various meetings, I attended in company with other ministers. During the same period I secured over $4000 for the salaries of other brethern. In the month of May, 1870, I decided, for reasons entirely satisfactory to my own mind, to join the Benicia presbytery of the Presbyterian church. It is not necessary to state these reasons here but will only say that I have never regretted the choice I made. The first year I was with them I accepted of the colporture work, selling the books of the board of publication. Rev. S. T. Wells had charge of the board's publications for several years and it was at his request I went to work. My first trip was up the coast as far as Mendocino City and through the mountains to Little Lake valley and down past Ukiah, Cloverdale and Healdsburg. There was preaching held at various places and some localities I found entirely destitute and very desirous to have services. One place I remember they offered, if Presbyterians would send them a minister, to give him $600 a year at that point and there were other places in reach where very near as much more could be secured. It was only a few years after this until the sawmill at the main point ceased to operate and business became very dull and now it looks like an old deserted miner's town. In making that journey I came to Point Arena one day about noon and decided to dine at the hotel. When I stepped into the barroom a man (I can hardly call him a gentleman) said, "Come up, stranger, and let us have a dram together."

"No, sir, I never went to a public bar in my life yet and had a horn and I do not propose to start in now."

"Sir, how long have you been in California," he asked.

When I told him he immediately said "you are a liar; no man ever lived in California that long without going to a bar for a drink."

I told him it did not matter whether he believed me or not, that I had told him the truth.

"No sir, you are a liar I tell you for I know the people of this state too well to believe anything of the kind. Come, now, my good fellow let us have a horn together."

I then told him and a number of others, the bartender included, that all men would be better off financially and morally if they would let liquor alone. This seemed to irritate him and he came near enough to shake his fist under my nose. I suppose he thought he would scare me as I was among strangers and he among his drinking friends. I laughed at him and told him I met on this coast a man of his kind almost every day of my life and that I was not by any means alarmed when they made such approaches as he did. A man standing by, and calling him by name, said, "Let that man alone, for he looks like a gentleman and I believe he has told you the truth.

This drew his attention for the time from me and just then the dinner bell was ringing and I went to my meal and saw nothing more of him. No doubt he would have done better had he been sober. There are men who drink, who, when sober, are nice and gentlemanly and I have no doubt but this man was one of that kind.

North of Point Arena six miles I tarried several days selling books and preaching in the school house at night. Little did I then think I would ever become a settled pastor in that region of country and remain there for years, preaching the gospel, visiting the sick, marrying the young people and burying the dead, but such proved to be the fact in after years. That matter, however, I will present in its appropriate place and speak further about the journey. During this trip a Southern Methodist minister was my traveling companion and after we left Mendocino City the large timber along our way greatly interested him. Once we come in sight of an enormous redwood tree growing in a little flat not far from our road and he wanted to measure it. He went down and stepped around that tree and after making all allowances he decided it was twenty-five feet in diameter. He was amazed at its size and in fact I had never found one so large before although I had been in California some time. After measuring it we wanted to determine its height as near as we could. We concluded it was at least 200 feet to the lowest limb and at least 150 feet to the top branch from that limb, making the tree 350 feet. When I was in the states in 1873 (this is what we call our old homes out here) I visited a sister who had several sons who were studying mathematics and I told

them that I saw one tree in California that would
fence in their entire farm of 32 acres and div de it off
into forty acre lots and build them a good house and
barn. "Uncle," they exclaimed, "if we did not know
you to be a truthful man we could not possibly believe
that story."

"Well," said I, "you can have a test of it giving the
size and height of the tree. Now, saw off the butt cut
and take one-eighth of it and see how many pickets it
would make 1x4 inches, six feet long.

They had only figured a little while when they exclaimed, "It will fence two such places and build two
houses and barns."

There is a large church in Santa Rosa built entirely
from one tree and it a very small one compared to the
one we saw. We have a perfect right to speak of large
things in this state for they are realities. Even our taxes
are enormously large with but little to show for them.
We are a long ways ahead of most of the states for we
even tax churches, making them pay whether they have
an income sufficient or not. After we left the big tree
we found we were not going to be able to reach Little
Lake valley that night and that we were out in the
mountains without a house to be seen or a blanket to
shield us from the cold, for it was the month of October
and quite chilly, and no grass for our horses and not a
match to strike fire with. We pressed on until after
sundown when we came to the crossing of Big river and
there we found about thirty people out on a picnic.
They had been there several days and had caught a fine
lot of trout and killed a number of deer. They came

from Mendocino City and were well supplied with provisions. I selected the man who I thought was the leader and as I had some California brass in my face, at least more than my traveling companion, who had only been in the state a few months, I walked up to him and required, "Can we stay all night with you, for we are caught here without food or blankets. We expected to make Little Lake but we cannot do it."

"Certainly, gentleman, just walk in and make yourselves at home."

The man whom I approached first said, "Ladies, stand back, for I am going to get these gentleman their supper; they have been traveling all day without any thing to eat and are very hungry."

We unharnessed the tea and he said, "there is plenty of hay; you will not find any grass near here so help yourselves."

Soon it was announced that supper was ready and as good a one as any one need want. We had trout and venison for meat and we had pie and take, with tea in abundance. After the supper was over they arranged for the children a kind of sabbath school concert and theater mixed and had the exercises interspersed with some good music. Among the singers my traveling companion sang a solo to their great delight and amusement. The wild woods echoed and reechoed with the evening's entertainment and even the owls joined in the chorus, saying, "who, who, haw at us." It had been a green spot to me in life's pilgrimage ever since. It was truly a night of real rich enjoyment. The next morning I thought that it would be nothing but right to pay

them for their trouble, but, no, they would not hear to
it and we thanked them kindly and the leader said,
"gentlemen, if you ever pass this way again and find us
here you will be perfectly welcome to remain over night
with us."

"A friend in need is a friend indeed," so says the old
adage and we found it so that night with all the good
things they gave us, for it was not only plenty for ourselves and horses but also a good bed on which to rest
I have often wished I had a picture of that camp just as
as it was that night in the wild woods of Mendocino
county. I can still see that pleasant company and how
the children enjoyed the evening as well as older people
I can see the vension hanging to the trees and the nice
trout in pans ready for the morning's meal. I can still
see that merry company as they would occasionally burst
out in laughter at the comical speech of some child and
greet it with rousing cheers. I believe it is true "that a
little fun now and then is relished by the best of men."
No one wants to go with a long sad face always as
though the Lord had forgotten them and the last friend
they had on earth was either dead or about to die. God
never intended us to go all the time with long and solemn faces but he wants us to enjoy life in a sensible way
and with it be joyful to him. There are times when sad-
ness enters the heart and the design is that we may be
benefitted by it but we can be greatly benefitted by our
times of joy and of rejoicing as well.

The next place we came to of much importance was
Little Lake valley, a valley out in the mountains surrounded with timber. Here we tarried for the Sabbath

and preached for them, the Baptists kindly giving us
the use of their church. They have now quite a village
in the valley called Willits. In its early history this
valley witnessed some terrible tragedies, one in which
six or seven men were killed in one day, but these days
are passed and the civilizing and refining influences of
the gospel has come among the inhabitants to remain
and lift them up and to·stay with them so they can and
will appreciate life.

After returning home I made another journey to Calistoga, a town situated at the head of Napa valley in
Napa county. Here they had no minister but were very
anxious to have preaching. I also went to Tomales on
the coast in Marin county and found they had a good
church building, but no one to preach in it. I resigned
my work as colporture and resolved to devote all my
energies to the two places above named. It was not long
until there was a church organized at Calistoga and a
subscription started for a church building. After a few
month's work there I gave that point up to the brother
occupying St. Helena as Tomales had decided that I
must preach there every Sabbath There was no church
organized, neither a Sabbath school and when the trustees were about to make arrangements for permanent
work they told me there was a debt of $2500 on the
building. They had built one house and it had burned
down and in building the second one they were involved
in the amount named above. They said they wanted
me to know how things were and then I would know
better what to do and how to manage. These trustees,
without any exception, were not members of the church

but good business men to work with. I told them I was
very hard to discourage when I entered on a work with
a full and clear understanding. "Now," said I, "will
you take hold and work with me until that debt is paid."
They said they would. The house had never been dedi-
cated. I wrote to Mr. Hemphill, now Dr. Hemphill, to
come up and preach the sermon, which he did, and after
the sermon there was more than $1600 secured by sub-
scriptions and cash. Then the church erection board
gave $600 and the trustees managed the remainder so
that it was soon announed that the church was out of
debt. I should have said that before this we organized
a church, with I think, fifteen members and also a Sabbath school had been organized and was doing good
work. There was no parsonage and all said, "let us
build one and then our work will be more permanent, as
our minister will then live with us."

The ladies held a fair and festival and cleared $1100
and I got all the hauling necessary promised, together
with a good reduction on the price of lumber. It was
not long until the parsonage was completed and the parson and his family in it.

At the spring meeting of presbytery in 1873 I was appointed as commissioner to the general assembly, which
met in Baltimore.

After I decided to preach every Sabbath at Tomales
and finding there was so many of them engaged in dairy-
ing they concluded that an evening appointment would
not suit them and that I could be free to go where I
pleased. I established an afternoon appointment at
Bloomfield, seven miles away, and kept it up while I

continued to preach at Tomales. It was never my privilege to preach to a more whole-souled people than I found at Tomales. They were willing to pay a good salary, and were regular in their attendance at church whether they were members or not. During my stay of three years among them I think there were about twenty-five additions to the church and the debt paid and a parsonage built.

I went to Bloomfield after leaving Tomales. There was a fine church building, which was erected mainly by a Mr. Henry Hall (who was not a member of the church at the time) but was not finished inside All of the members who lived there were then connected with the Big Valley church at Valley Ford, four miles away, but has since been organized into a seperate church. It was not long until the church was finished and all seemed to rejoice in it. A short time after we moved to Bloomfield, a Catholic friend of mine said to me, "I want to ask you a question and I would like to have it answered."

"Yes," I said, "I will answer it with the greatest of pleasure, if I can."

He then said, "When you lived and preached at Tomales the people all kept sober on the Sabbath and were very orderly, but when we (that is the Catholics) had services, they were drinking and sometimes we had fights and occasionally a horse race. We never had the good order you did. Now, I want to know why there was that difference in the order of the two days."

"I suppose you want me to give you an honest answer."

"Certainly, I do."

"I know of no other reason than this, that our religion and the morals we advocate are better than yours."

Said he, "I will be equally honest and will say that I believe you have told the truth. Many a Sunday have I watched your people and seen their good deportment and know that it far surpassed ours."

For five years and a half while I preached at Bloomfield I also preached every two weeks at the Dunham school house or Stony Point. While living at Bloomfield there was a series of meeting held, not by evangelists, but the local pastors and one Sunday we received twenty-six into the church. Had it not been for the many removals there would have been a strong church there numerically but they have gone to various portions of the state until now there are but few left to support it. It was difficult then to manage finances and now it is much more difficult, having all been caused by deaths and removals, but the field, with all these drawbacks, is still occupied and it is fondly hoped the efforts will yet be crowned with success. I think during my stay of seven years (that is preaching there seven years) there were about forty accessions to the church.

The spring of 1879 a small church, which had been previously organized at Point Arena, requested me to visit them with the object in view of a permanent pastorate. I went and held a meeting for them and as matters were arranged satisfactory I decided to move there. There were difficulties to overcome that I had never encountered before. The minister who preceeded me had not acted as a minister of the gospel should and this,

together with the drinking habit of the people, made it
a hard field but I resolved to try it in the strength of
him who said, "I will never leave nor forsake thee."
The field was about thirty miles long reaching up and
down the coast, up as far as Bridgeport and down as far
as Gualala. I found it very hard work traveling on the
coast for sometimes the wind blew so hard that it would
send the gravel flying into my face until it would sting
with pain. In order to supply the field I had to preach
frequently three times on Sunday and travel thirty
miles. The church had no house of worship in all the
field. They did own a parsonage but it was in an un-
finished condition. There were foundations to be laid
and houses both spiritual and temporal to be erected
and it was expected that the parson would at least lead
the way in the temporalities of the church as well as in
its spiritual affairs. I commenced preaching in Point
Arena, May 1st, 1879, and was installed as pastor in
June of the same year. Services were held in a small
room in town, too small to accomodate those who wished
to attend, and it was not long until we purchased the
lower story of the Masonic hall and it was fitted up for
church purposes and is still in use. I found the people
in my new field of labor ready and willing to respond to
the calls made upon them for money to carry on church
work. At Manchester the Methodists had a house of
worship as well as at Point Arena but the Presbyterians
had always occupied the school house, why I did not
know. When I commenced work there the Methodists
wanted me to occupy the church and the Presbyterians
the school house and both parties came to me about the

matter and I told them I had nothing to say about it,
that I did not come there to enter into a quarrel the first
thing, that I was employed by the Presbyterians to
preach to them and if they said the preaching should be
in the school house or under a pine tree that was the
place where I was going. They voted unanimously for
the school house and as long as I preached for them
services were held there. Since I left them they have
built a neat church and seem to be quite prosperous. At
Bridgeport services have always been held in a school
house. At Gualala we commenced in a hall that was
used for politicial purposes and dancing, good templars,
etc. It was not long until there was a small neat church
erected through the influence of Mr. and Mrs. Hayward,
they paying for the most of it. Mr. H. was one of the
principal owners of the mill and saw the good influence
churches had on the men in his employ.

The time had been when at the mills and logging
camps hundred of men had been employed but all the
mills of that portion of the country extending from
Gualala to Bridgeport are now closed, save the one at
Gualala. This one still seems to be prosperous and
there is still an immense body of redwood and pine up
the river that can be floated down.

The greatest draw back to church work in that field
I found to be the rum power. Men were bold and im-
pudent and some of them made fortunes selling whiskey.
Sunday was the great drinking and gambling day of the
week and in some places they would get to much of old
"tanglefoot" in them as to get mad and they would return home with many a bruise disfiguring their faces. I

do not want by any means to leave the impression that
all the people living along the coast were in the habit of
drinking and gambling, for there were those who did
not drink at all and then there were families who feared
God and walked uprightly in the midst of their evil surroundings and these were the ones who helped the
country and built it up in morals. But under such influences it required the courage of a grizzly bear and
plenty of divine grace to stand up and say, "I am for
God and the good of my country." Even some ministers
who had gone among them gave way in an evil hour and
drifted with the multitude, and at least one filled a
drunkard's grave. Now things have changed to a certain
extent and there is not as much drinking and gambling
as formerly and the people will compare favorably in
morals with some older settled portions of our state. It
is true there are not as many men there as formerly but
those who are still there are inclined to that which is
right, with a much firmer grip than they were a number of years ago.

I remember that not a great while after I moved there
I was going into town one day from my study and had
to pass a saloon. In front of that saloon a number of
men were standing who had been drinking. Just as I
got opposite to them one of them said, "Boys, here is
the Parson, lets make him drink."

I looked up at him and said, "Sir, you will have a
sorry old time before you get through with that job."

"Boys, I tell you we had better let him alone for
their is fire in his eyes," said the speaker.

With one single exception I was treated kindly by

those who sold and those who drank. There was once that two men gambled a day and two nights and the second morning they got mad and one of them shot the other, it was thought at the time fatally, as the ball entered his body and could not be found. After lingering a long time and hovering between life and death he commenced to improve and finally seemed to be quite well. The bartender, who waited on them with liquor and watched their gambling and saw the shooting, gave me all the particulars and I wrote them down and sent them to a Petaluma paper and they were published and given to the world. About six months after this the one who did the shooting was in Petaluma and one of his friends said to him, "Who is writing you up at the Point."

He said, "No one that I knew of."

The article was given to him to read and when he returned home he made efforts to find out the author of it. He had accused several men, but all denied having written it. One evening just before sundown I went to the saddle shop on an errand. I had not been there very long when the one who did the shooting came in and I saw at a glance that he was drinking. He came where I was exclaiming, "Did you write it, did you write it."

I told him I did not understand what he meant.

"I mean, sir, that article in a Petaluma paper about me shooting a certain man."

"Yes, sir," said I, "I believe I wrote an article of that kind."

I had no thought of being struck by him, when all of a sudden he opened his hand and slapped me on the side of my face. The first thought that entered my mind was what would the Savior do under such circumstances, and I said to myself, "He would not strike back and I will not either." At that the saddler bounded to his feet and said, "I do not allow any man to strike a minister in my shop."

The lick he gave me only stunned me a little and made my head ache. When the saddler said what he did I told him to hold on and I would manage him, that all such men were cowards and I was not in the least alarmed. When I accused him of being a coward he commenced to feel for his pistol and I knew he always went armed. I said to him "Take your hand off from that pistol or you will get hurt badly."

There was a large saddler's hammer close to me and had he attempted my life with his pistol I should have used it on him. When I told him to take his hand off he did as I told him and I was glad of it for I had no desire to do him bodily harm. I then commenced and told him that he had with his saloon business and gambling ruined more young men along this coast than any other man who ever lived on it and that unless he changed his ways he was sure of a drunkard's hell and a drunkard's grave. Then again he began to feel for his pistol and I repeated my request that he take his hand off from it or he would be hurt badly and that very quick. He took his hand away the second time and I then told him, "You have been called the king along the coast and the bully just because you went armed and men knew it and they dreaded any trouble with you for fear they would be shot and killed or crippled for life,

Pat delivering the potatoes.—see page 154.

but you have found one man, sir, who does not dread your presence nor care for the arms you at times have with you."

At this onset he commenced to feel for his pistol again and I said, "take your hand off, and now understand I am not going to make another request of the kind and if you put that hand for the pistol again you will have to run the risk of what follows.

I then told him, "your wife and daughters I respect and will do any good I can for either you or your family. That I always pitied a man who got into the habit of drinking until he had no courage to quit. That the only thing or power in the universe which could save him was the Lord Jesus Christ; his grace and his alone could conquer and make a better man out of him."

At that time I saw his chin begin to quiver and the tears to start and he held out his hand, saying, "Shan't we be good friends from this on."

Said I, "Sir, I court no man's friendship, but if I can have it on high and honorable terms I am willing to accept of it, but not otherwise."

Said he, "I promise I will never do you any harm as long as I live; you will be my friend."

"Yes," I told him "I will."

When I returned home my wife asked what kept me so late. I told her what had transpired and for the first and last time in her life she said, "Oh, let us move away from such an ungodly place."

"No," said I, "not as long as I have strength to work. I am going to stand in the strength of the Lord and fight the devil in his own den."

It produced quite an excitement in town and one of my friends said he would have given the Parson twenty dollar if he had just let in and have given him a good thrashing. Then he studied a moment and said, "No, he did the best deed of his life not to touch him."

This man, although he was one of the main property owners of the town, did not live there long after that, for the men were all the time picking at him and saying, "well, you found one man, if he was a preacher, who was not afraid of you and I tell you you had better be on the lookout for him."

He moved up the coast some distance and afterwards in company with a friend I went up there on a missionary tour. While there I learned he was very sick at the hotel and that his recovery was very doubtful. I went over to see him, and, really, I do not know whether he was glad to see me or not. I found him confined to his bed and when I took a seat and commenced to talk with him he was not so sick but what he knew enough to put his arm between his eyes and my face and then either peep over or under his arm at me. Poor fellow. I have often thought of what men used to say about him, "That he would die yet with his boots on." He was thrown from his buggy and killed.

There was in Point Arena a house of bad repute and the inmate was taken very sick and her doctor thought she was sure to die and he left her and went into the mountains. She became greatly alarmed and sent for another doctor who was a good christian man and he frankly told her he had but little hopes for her recovery and that if she wanted to talk with a minister she had better send for one soon. "Oh," she said, "they would not come here knowing the life I have led."

The doctor said, "Yes, my Pastor and his wife will both come, I have no doubt of it."

She sent for us and we went and she said, "As a minister 1 was afraid you would not come."

I told her 1 regarded it the duty of a minister to go wherever he could do good and save the people.

She then said, "1 want you to read some scripture and pray with me."

"What will you have read," 1 inquired, "about the woman whom Christ did not condemn and asked her where her accusers were" she replied.

1 read that and other portions of the scripture that 1 thought would suit her case such as "Come unto me all ye that labor, are heavy laden and 1 will give you rest." Finally 1 said, "Are you willing, here and now, to say 1 will quit my evil ways and trust the Lord Jesus Christ for the salvation of my soul and live for his glory while 1 live."

With the very deepest emotion of soul, she said, "Yes, 1 will," and her countenance indicated a great change and 1 bowed with her in prayer and from that time on she began to mend and when the other doctor returned he went to see her and she told him, "Dr. B. is going to care for my body and the Lord Jesus Christ has saved my soul and 1 shall have no further need of you."

She recovered and married not long after her recovery and, as far as I ever heard, kept her promise. She told me she was raised in the midst of plenty and never had to work for a living. After her marriage she went with her husband to Colorado and there he deserted her and she was left without a dollar in the world. She had married contrary to her parents' wishes and was both ashamed and afraid to ask for help when her husband left her. No doubt her parents would have given her a helping hand had she asked for it, for they were members of the Episcopal church, and, she said, good christian people. But shame and confusion of face was her lot and rather than say, "I have done wrong and ask your forgiveness," she decided on a life very different, but was finally arrested in her downward career, and, let us hope, repented of it all.

I remained at and near Point Arena nine years and eight months, and while there I married sixty couple, baptised eighty-four, buried nine-three persons, received into the communion of the church, fifty-seven members. After preaching there so long it affected my throat and eyes until I was compelled to cease my life's work and rest, at least for awhile. I was placed by act of presbytery on the Honorably Retired List and since 1889 have not asked for a church to preach to for I have not been able. I have preached occasionally in some destitute places near home.

While I lived at Point Arena I went once to attend a meeting of presbytery at Vallejo and when I arrived in San Francisco I found that Rev. Mr. Hammond was holding a series of meetings there and as I had some time to spend before the presbytery met, and had never heard him, concluded to attend. It so happened that he was absent at the time and I did not get to hear him until the next evening at Vallejo. However, there was a very good sermon preached in keeping with revival efforts. After the conclusion of the sermon there was a general inquiry meeting held in which a number of ministers and members engaged. I think the inquiry meeting resulted in a great deal of good. It was conducted by those who knew what they were doing and as they went from one to another the interest seemed to increase. Finally one of the ministers who was at work, a Rev. Mr. Tables, came where I was seated and asked, "are you a christian?"

I told him I sometimes thought when I heard others talk that I might be and then again when I heard some others talk was not so sure about it. I told him I had a great desire to be religious and serve God.

"You ought, sir, to have more than a passing desire to that effect, it ought to burn down into your soul with such power that you would know for yourself and not another that you have passed from death unto life. There ought to be such earnestness that you would cry out, 'God be merciful to me a sinner.' 'Lord save or I perish.'"

"Yes," I asked, "is there not danger of becoming unduly excited and by that means make a mistake and that mistake result in very serious consequences."

"There is no danger, as a general thing, of one of mature years being mistaken. There is," said he, "no necessity for one to make a great noise about religion, for deep water always runs silent while the shallow makes a great noise. My friend," continued he, "it becomes you to be deeply in earnest about this matter and not postpone it any longer or you may lose your soul and be eternally lost."

"I want then to know, sir, in a very plain, simple manner, how 1 am to be saved, for is there not a very great mystery connected with the thought of a sinful being approaching infiinte purity and begging for pardon. Will not such a being spurn one from his presence and send me to the world of woe? "

" No, God tells us, ' He that cometh to me I will in no wise cast out ; ' 'The prodigal son returned to his father's house although clad in rags.' "

" Even if he should receive me, I would like to know how to come to him. Had I not better wait until I make myself more uneasy about my present condition or then wait for a convenient season? "

" You will never find a better time than now—and you are sufficiently uneasy about your condition. You can come to him now without a moment's delay. Now is the accepted time, behold, now is the day of salvation. Now God's people are ready to pray for you and assist you in coming to Christ. Jesus even now stands with out-stretched arms ready to receive you. This name is worthy with the Father and for His sake he will have mercy on you and save you."

"Yes, but after I have believed, how am I to know I am saved, for I do not want any mistakes about it."

"In the first place, He said the Holy Spirit will bear witness with your Spirit that you are a child of God and have passed from death unto life."

" Then if you have passed from death unto life you will love all who bear the image of the Saviour."

"You can also tell by the desires you have. If any are made Christians and bear Christ's image they have a great desire that others be saved and enjoy the religion of Christ with them. The regenerated soul longs to see God's glory among men."

One other question, "Am I to expect that I can live right at all time and have so much help from the Holy Spirit that I will not sin against Him if I become a child of God.'

"The Scriptures tell us, ' No man liveth and sinneth not,' but if any man sin we have an advocate with the Father, even Jesus Christ, the righteous."

'' There is one point more I would like to understand. Is there any more safety for the soul after it is really saved than before? When I invest money I want to know that it is safe, and certainly I would want to know whether I will be any more secure after than before in religious matters ? "

" Yes," he said, " It is God's work and His alone when a soul is saved and He declares, 'their sins and iniquities will I remember no more;' which hope we have as an anchor of the soul, both sure and steadfast. ' My Grace shall be sufficient for thee.' "

" You seem to have some knowledge of the Scriptures."

" I was reared in a pious family, where the Bible was read at family worship."

"You seem to understand something, too, of the plan of salvation."

" Yes, I have been in the habit of attending church and hearing that plan explained more or less."

" Now, allow me to ask you your name ? "

" It does not matter so much about my name as it

does about being a child of God, and trying to get to heaven."

"Yes, but please tell me your name."

He begged so hard that I finally told him.

"What!" while astonishment covered his face, "not C. H. Crawrord, a Presbyterian minister."

"Yes, sir, the same man."

"Well, I have nothing more to say to you at present, only this, I have been in the state a number of years and ever since I have been here I have heard of you as one of the pioneers who has led many souls to Christ."

CHAPTER XXIX.

During a missionary tour, once, I learned where an old Illinois friend lived, and as I had not seen him for many years, I concluded to call on him. When I arrived at his house and was cordially greeted by him and his family, he asked me, "will you preach at our school house to-night, if I circulate an appointment?"

I told him I would—that preaching was all I pretended to follow.

"You will have some to preach too, to night, who declare themselves infidels."

At the hour appointed there was a goodly number assembled for a small community. The subject for the evening was showing the advantages which Christianity had over all the systems of infidelity. When I closed the discourse I asked all who believed that Christianity had advantage over infidelity, to rise to their feet. The entire congregation rose, except two young men. I then called on any present who believed that any system of infidelity was better than Christianity to manifest it by rising to their feet. All remained seated and as silent as the grave.

After the congregation was dismissed, one of the young men, who did not vote for Christianity, came shaking his fist under my nose, and saying, "you, sir, are not a gentleman."

" When you say that you make a very serious accusation against a minister of gospel—for of all men he ought certainly to be a gentleman as well as a true Christian. What, sir, is the matter with you? I do not understand why you make such a charge as that."

" You had no business to take such a vote as you did."

" Oh, that is the trouble is it, you are an infidel, and ashamed to own it, and ashamed to vote for it in public. If you are ashamed of your principles you had better get away from them, for fear they will be your ruin."

" You are a stranger to me," said he, " but I must advise you to never take such a vote as that again, while you live for fear you might get a tremendous thrashing."

" I am not in the least afraid of that for that is business two can take a hand in. When I know I am in the right it always make me brave, so that I do not fear the face of man. But, now, my friend, seriously, would you not rather trust Christianity for safety, than any system of infidelity ? "

His reply was, " I would not." A reply he would not have made had he not been mad. At that we parted, and I have never met him since that night. The friend whom I went to see was well acquainted with him and

he told me that not long after this he made profession of
religion and had sent word to me through him, "that
he would give me $10 for every sermon I would come
and preach to him."

I have found in my experience that it is sometimes an
excellent plan to make some men mad and then when
the passion wears off, they will see in their calm
moments how foolish they have been and turn to the
only true source of help. This man was not the first
one by any means whom I have seen leave meetings
mad and the result was they returned in deep penitence
and sought forgiveness of the One who alone can forgive
sins.

I made another missionary trip, this time into the Sierra
Nevada mountains of which I will speak. About sun-
down I found a village with a few hundred inhabitants in
it—and the first one in all my western travels without a
hotel. How this happened I can not tell, for somebody
is almost sure to keep a public house even if it is a poor
one. But let the house be ever so poor, the price is
always good, (that is good for the keeper's pocket.) I
drove up to a store and inquired for a stopping place.
The gentleman said, "their is none in town, but I can
take care of your horse, and there is a boarding and
lodging house kept not far away and there you can
get something to eat, but you will have to sleep on the
floor and wrap yourself in the blankets, they will furnish as the best that can be done."

After the horse was cared for I went into the store
and to my astonishment, found the owner was selling
"tangle-foot" as well as dry goods and groceries. Dur-
our conversation I asked him if they ever had any
preaching in the town. He told me he had lived there
a good many years, in fact was one of the first to settle
there and to his certain knowledge there had been only
three sermons preached in the place. "Do you preach?"
he asked.

"Yes, sir, that is my business."

"Will you preach tonight if I get you a congregation?"

I told him I would. I went to the boarding house for my meal and he started out notifying the people. They had a very large school house and at the appointed hour it was full and all the windows had lockers on. I never preached to a more attentive audience anywhere. I found something to eat and slept on the hard floor and the next morning the merchant who kept my horse told me that "at home in the state of Maine he always went with his mother and sister to church twice on Sunday and to Sabbath school and they had no idea how bad he was out here, and for the world he did not want them to know he was selling whiskey."

He furnished all the lights for the school house and paid all my bills, with a promise given of reformation but whether this took place I cannot tell.

CHAPTER XXX.

When I was living and preaching at Point Arena in Mendocino county, California, there was one time when at the close of the conference year the Methodists found they were behind with what they had promised to give their minister and that it was necessary to do something so as to meet their obligations. The matter was talked over among themselves and the decision was to hold a church social with ice cream and cake as an "accompaniment" as musicians say. A wise man always provides for the wants of both soul and body and these church socials properly conducted do the same thing. The basement of the church being quite large it proved a good room for these socials, for as a rule there are more who will attend a social than a preaching appointment. The first of the week I saw Mr. Adams, the pastor of the church, and he gave me a very cordial and pressing invitation to be present, remarking at the same time, "you have a good deal of mischief and fun about you; I wish you would open the exercises Thursday night with some of it."

At the appointed time 1 went and found the room filled with an anxious, good-natured company. In arranging the room they had placed a stand with some nice bouquets on it and I was to stand behind it to make my remarks. At the appointed time Mr. A. motioned to me and we took our places, when he said to them, "Mr. C. has been here so long he does not need any formal introduction for they all knew me and he hoped 1 would begin right away as the people were especially anxious, he knew, about the eating part of the social."

When I begun I told them this was a strange world of strange things in which we lived. Pointing to the beautiful flowers before me 1 said, "look at those bouquets, they are of all colors and yet they have the same soil in which to grow, the same air and the same sunshine, yet, strange to say, they are not all one color nor yet are they the same size. When we go forth to life's duties and walk or drive along the public highway we find at almost every step strange things. Look at the trees of the forest, how strange they are, some tower up towards the heavens while others are low and scrubby. Some are very small while others are of immense size and yet with all this no two leaves of the forest are precisely alike. Strange they were not all made alike in their trunks and their leaves. Then there are the stars that are such strange things, some of them are large and others small, some shine a great deal more brilliantly than others. 'Twinkle, twinkle little star, how I wonder what you are, up above the world so high like a diamond in the sky.' These brilliant orbs are all strange things to us. Then there is the sun, one of the most wonderful of strange objects on which our visions light.

It has been giving off both light and heat for thousands of years past and still seems to have an inexhaustible suppy left. It is a strange object, set in the heavens by Omnipotent power.

After speaking of all these strange things in nature I then said, with as much emphasis as I was master of, "But of all the strange things in this world of strange things, the strangest thing is when a Methodist minister calls on a Presbyterian minister to do some solid begging for him, when it is known in all communities where they work side by side that the Methodist can outbeg the Presbyterians two to one."

At this unexpected sally they stamped their feet and clapped their hands at a very lively rate and when they saw it made Mr. Adams blush they renewed it time and again. When I finished my remarks I took a seat by the side of Mr. A. and he shook his fist at me very good-naturedly and said, loud enough for all to hear, "I will pay you for that my good brother." At this they renewed their cheering.

The evening was a real social one and everybody seemed to enjoy themselves. Mr. A. told me a few days after this that his social was a decided success and that what I said was the means of his getting at least twenty-five dollars which he would not have had had I not made that speech. I told him I was glad of it for I loved to be useful outside of my own church and home.

It is very often the case that small country churches have a very hard struggle to keep out of debt and keep their finances well in hand. A church debt is to be dreaded a great deal more than private debts. In private debts as a rule there is but one person to worry about it but in church debts every true member feels that they are responsible for a just proportion of what is due. But of all connected with the church I think the pastor feels the burden of a debt more than any one else. I remember when we purchased one-half of the Masonic building at Point Arena for a church that we became involved and it took quite an effort to pay it off. Finally the work was accomplished and I told them from the pulpit one Sunday that our debt was all paid and the church so far as finances were concerned was free. A very shrewd, intelligent man of the word, who had made an excellent success of his own business affairs, said to me the next day, "you have but little idea how much power their was in those few words you spoke yesterday about the church being free from debt, for church debts keep people from joining and becoming identified with the church's interest. You may expect your church to prosper from this on."

If this was the prophecy of a man of the world it has came as true as Balaam's prophecy did, for from a mere handful of members then it has grown to number at the present time 165   The prospects are still good for a future growth and greater usefullness. I certainly will ever retain a kindly rememberance of the people living along the coast from Gualala to Bridgeport, for many years I shared their hospitality and have been with numbers of them in their times of sorrow, when their dead were laid gently away to await the sound of the trump of God at the last day.

I love the state in which I live and for the last forty years have tried to advance its best interests by opposing the evil and advocating the good and I want still to see it rising as a mighty giant along the borders of the great Pacific and standing as the beacon light amid the cluster of states which bedecks our western horizon. If anything I have said in this book shall help in these matters I shall be satisfied.